The

TEX-BONE: Triple Option for the 21st Century

Joe Austin

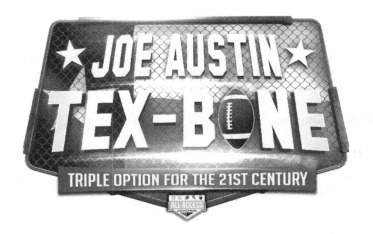

The Tex-Bone: Triple Option for the 21st Century
First Edition, January 2021
ISBN 9798584752361
Copyright © 2021 by Joe Austin

Ordering Information:
Special discounts are available on quantity purchases by corporations, associations, and others, especially educational uses for faculty, staffs, and schools. Special editions or book excerpts can also be created to meet specific needs.

Printed in the United States of America by All Access Publishing.

Ordering Information:

Special discounts are available on quantity purchases by corporations, associations, and others, especially educational uses for faculty, staffs, and schools. Special editions or book excerpts can also be created to meet specific needs.

Printed in the United States of America

All Access Coaching:

Websites

> www.allaccesscoaching.com
> www.allaccesscamps.com
> www.coachjoeaustin.com

Videos

Tex Bone: Overview	Tex Bone: G Load Pass
Tex Bone: Power Option	Tex Bone: Double Pull Power Pro
Tex Bone: G Load Option	Tex Bone: Power Read Pro
Tex Bone: Double Pull Power	Tex Bone: Iso Pass
Tex Bone: Speed Option	Tex Bone: Perimeter & Wing Blocking
Tex Bone: Power Read	Tex Bone: Offensive Line Blocking
Tex Bone: Veer Option	Tex Bone: RB & QB Drills
Tex Bone: Isos & Counters	Tex Bone: Practice Organization
Tex Bone: Power Option Pass	T Tex Bone: Game Planning & Game Day

DEDICATION

As I began this project I prayed to my God that He would bless this work and that it would glorify Him. I continue to dedicate this work to Him by, "Being confident that He who has begun a good work in us will carry it on to completion until the day of Jesus Christ." (Philippians 1:6). Mahalo ke akua nui loa.

My wife, Marissa, allows me to invest countless hours into my vocation. I will forever be grateful for her love, support and friendship. She is my best friend and this book is dedicated to her. My daughter, Reagan Lililehua, has learned that she must share her Daddy with our ohana at the "football factory", which is what she calls my work. That ohana is our players and coaches and their families. I appreciate her willingness to share her Daddy and I dedicate this book to her. I hope our time at the beach house and our Friday morning trips for hash browns at Mickey D's is able to make up for the nights that I'm not home to kiss her goodnight and read her books.

This book is dedicated to my family. My brother, Dr. Ryan Austin, has not only been a supporting older brother, but he was integral in the editing and compilation of this book. He is, after all, the scholar of the family. The man holds five college degrees! He logged many hours in cleaning up the first draft of this book and this work wouldn't be what it is without him. My parents, Dan and Deb, have always supported me as I searched for my passion – which, outside of my family, is football. They have made a lot of sacrifices on my behalf and this has created a debt that I can never repay. They always encouraged me to pursue a career where my work wouldn't really be work. My Uncle Bill texts me every day. He has also been a source of support and encouragement for my entire life, as has my Aunt Nancy.

I have been blessed to work with some tremendously talented and dedicated coaches and players. This book is dedicated to them for everything that they have taught me over the first twenty years of my coaching career. I have learned more from Coach Tom Ross, the co-creator of the Tex-Bone system, than any other coach. I am thankful that he granted me permission to take our offensive system and share it with the world. My name is on the book, but this is a team effort. Tom Ross is the only man I know in which about ten different people would all say that he is their best friend. I think that says all that needs to be said about Tom.

Coaches Kenneth Eboh and Bill Kriesel have had enough faith in me to move across the country to coach with me. In Kenneth's case, he has moved multiple times to multiple states. I will forever be grateful for their friendship and faith in me. I have equal, if not grater, faith in them. Chad Ellis and Nick Mask have joined our band along the way and have become tremendous friends. Thank you both.

It's a slippery slope to start mentioning players that have had an impact on my life, but I would be remiss not to mention some of the very talented quarterbacks that I have had the privilege of working with. Our time in the meeting room, where things are laid back and we can all be who we are, has produced some of the most cherished moments of my career. Here's to the quarterbacks that have made my career meaningful because of the relationship they sought to build with me: James McNear, Marcus Lavesseur, Jermar Jackson, CJ Croft, Dexter Britt, Bryan Hicks, and Fred Hover. There are certainly more players that have touched my life, but my space is limited to this page. I hope all of the players that I have coached know that they are special people to me.

In my adolescence I was molded as a football player and young man by two coaches: Tom Gruening and Joe McQuerry. Richard Bright was a teacher that was also very influential. This book is dedicated to these men.

Finally, this book is also dedicated to the memory of my dear friend, Merry Ross. We love and miss you.

Jeremiah 29:11

PREFACE

We were in the third quarter of my first game as a collegiate head coach. I was the head coach at Hanover College and we were playing Centre College; a very good team and a national playoff contender. They were loaded. We were starting eleven true freshmen. The game was going as you would expect.

Midway through the third quarter we had somehow matriculated the ball down to the Centre three yard line and had first and goal. Our young team responded by snapping the ball over the head of our quarterback making it second and goal from the 18 yard line.

In addition to being the head coach I was also the offensive coordinator. I looked down at my play sheet. Somewhere on this menu of options there must be the perfect call for second and goal from the 18 yard line. Right? There wasn't. I knew there wasn't, but I kept looking anyway.

The play clock was running down and the players were looking to me for the personnel, formation and play call.

At that moment there was a tap on my shoulder. A part-time assistant coach that I had inherited from the previous staff had done the tapping. When I turned to him he said, "Joe, the pizza delivery guy is here and wants to get paid."

That's football. It is so unpredictable that folks that aren't in our world can't even imagine the number of variables that affect victory or defeat. If you try to describe the number of variables that play into the success or failure of a football team most folks will quickly lose interest in the minutia.

This is not a book for those folks that lose interest in details. This is a book for the folks that love the minutia of football. Every now and then there is a team that is so physically dominant that they can roll out the ball and say, "Go get 'em boys!" I've played that team, but God has never called me to coach that team. If you haven't been called to coach that team I pray that this system will help you become a giant killer. In my first twenty years of coaching we have certainly taken down our share of teams that, on paper, we weren't supposed to beat.

It seems to me that when I started coaching 20 years ago our industry was more open to the exchange of information. When I attended clinics in the 90's there were presentations with a lot of game film and playbook diagrams. Now, it seems to me that most clinics are about philosophy or rudimentary schematics because coaches are scared to share their systems for fear of giving their opponents an advantage. Rest assured that I am not worried about that. Besides, in our league we share every game so my opponents know plenty about the Tex-Bone already. The purpose of this book is to place the Tex-Bone offensive system into the collective body of knowledge that is available to all coaches at all levels.

Joe Austin, August, 2019

TABLE OF CONTENTS

Dedication ii

Preface iii

Why The Tex-Bone? v

I. TEX-BONE OVERVIEW
    Ch 1: Philosophy & Structure 3
    Ch 2: Formation Families & Personnel 15
    Ch 3: Tempo, Backfields & Fullbacks 21
    Ch 4: Numbering System 31

II. RUN GAME
    Ch 5: Power Option 39
    Ch 6: G Load Option 51
    Ch 7: Double Pull Power 59
    Ch 8: Speed Option 69
    Ch 9: Power Read 77
    Ch 10: Veer Option 87
    Ch 11: Isos & Counters... 99

III. PASS GAME
    Ch 12: Power Option Pass 113
    Ch 13: G Load Pass 121
    Ch 14: Double Pull Power Pass 129
    Ch 15: Power Read Pass 137
    Ch 16: Iso Pass... 145

IV. COACHING THE TEX-BONE
    Ch 17: Wing & Perimeter Blocking............................. 153
    Ch 18: Offensive Line Blocking Drills.......................... 161
    Ch 19: Running Back, Quarterback & Receiver Drills....... 169
    Ch 20: System & Practice Organization 181
    Ch 21: Game Plan Considerations & Ready Lists 195
    Ch 22: Game Day 205

V. APPENDIX 209

WHY THE TEX-BONE?

The Tex-Bone is triple option for the 21st century. In this book you will learn how implement this new offense with your team. Everything to coach the players is included: playbook diagrams, rules, drills, coaching points, game planning and play calling strategies, etc.

So what is the Tex-Bone system?

The Tex-Bone system is the marriage of traditional triple option and the modern spread into one Texas-sized offense that leaves your opponent scrambling to cover it all.

The Tex-Bone features **two innovative strategies** for modern triple option execution: (1) the Tex-Bone is the first option system to feature the Power Run as the foundational scheme and (2) the Tex-Bone has made every formation imaginable a formation that can be used for executing option.

We still run option from the Flexbone, but that is just the tip of the iceberg. When teams run option for the Flexbone formation they are almost certain to face a defense designed specifically to counteract your offense. On the other hand, spread formations offer more predictable alignments. This means that you will likely have a very good idea as to how the defense you are facing will defend you. **This is the advantage of the Tex-Bone!** You can now run triple option with a high degree of certainty as to what you are up against: who will cover the dive, who will cover the quarterback and who will cover the pitch.

In addition to these **game planning and play calling advantages** the Tex-Bone features new advantages for triple option execution. For example, you will no longer need to motion your pitch player pre-snap. This is important because not motioning conceals the direction of your option play.

All of the **Tex-Bone schemes are rule based**, which means your players can be aggressive. In addition, players that are well versed in the Tex-Bone rules will not be thrown by slanting or shifting defenses and **blitz countermeasures are built in** to the schemes. These results can be achieved through what we call our **economy of techniques**. This means that only a hand full of individual skills are needed by each player to be able to execute the entire system.

WHAT'S IN THIS BOOK

In this book you will learn that this system is adaptable to your players and allows you to play to their strengths. We only ask our players to be in roles that suit their skills, and you can to. In addition, you will learn to choose the elements of the Tex-Bone system that are best for your team on a season to season or week to week basis.

Look at it this way: **the Tex-Bone is a tool box for coaches.** Every week or year you might use a different tool, but the system never changes.

If you have ever wanted a system that is hard to defend, moldable to your players and has all the answer built in the Tex-Bone is for you.

SECTION 1: Tex-Bone Overview

The study of the Tex-Bone system begins with a review of the history of option football. From there we dive into the philosophy and structural components of the system. The formation families, personnel, tempos, backfields actions and number system are all discussed.

SECTION 2: Run Game

Everything you need to master the Tex-Bone run game is contained in Section 2. In-depth explanation of the rules and techniques for each player on the field is outlined for all of the Tex-Bone run schemes:

- Power Option
- G Load Option
- Double Pull Power
- Speed Option
- Veer Option
- Isos & Counters

SECTION 3: Pass Game

The emphasis that opponents of the Tex-Bone must place on stopping the run leads to big plays in the pass game. Each Tex-Bone run has passes that compliment it:

- Power Option Pass
- G Load Pass
- Double Pull Power Pass
- Power Read Pass
- Iso Pass

SECTION 4: Coaching the Tex-Bone

Once you know the schemes, Section 4 outlines drills for each position. Great detail is paid to blocking technique for the perimeter and the offensive line. A systematic way to install triple option is detailed so even the most novice of triple option coaches can get the Tex-Bone up and running in just a few minutes.

The last chapters of the book prepare the offensive coordinator for administering the system and both pre-season and in-season duties are outlined. Finally, tips and strategies for game planning and play calling are discussed, as well as suggestions for organizing your coaching staff during practice and games.

TEX-BONE OVERVIEW

1. Philosophy & Structure
2. Formation Families & Personnel
3. Tempo, Backfields & Fullbacks
4. Numbering System

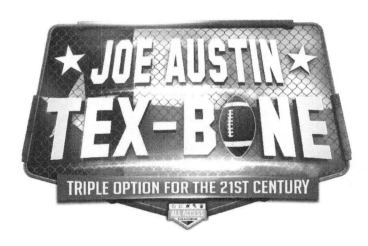

2

CH 1: PHILOSOPHY & STRUCTURE

Welcome to the Joe Austin Tex-Bone: Triple Option for the 21st century. The Tex-Bone was developed with Tom Ross, my coaching colleague of more than 15 years.

HISTORICAL OVERVIEW

Before we begin examining the Tex-Bone system it is important to look at the history of triple and double option football. Looking at its history reveals the origins of the Tex-Bone system.

The Split T

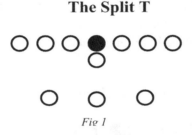

Fig 1

Option football dates back to the days of the Split T Formation (Figure 1) Don Farot used this set for the first time at the University of Missouri in 1941. Farot's development of option football was initially inspired by observations of "2 on 1" fast breaks in basketball. He liked the edge gained by the offensive team in two-on-one situations—especially when the offensive team scored a basket on almost every possession with the one-man advantage. Farot envisioned applying the concept of numerical advantage in basketball to offensive football. The University of Missouri secured the school's first Sugar Bowl invitation by going 8-2 that year using the new "option" offense.

The Wishbone

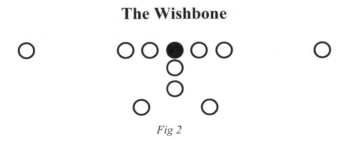

Fig 2

The next major innovation in option football was the Wishbone (Figure 2). The Wishbone was created at the University of Texas by assistant coach Emery Bellard. Putting this new offense into action was a potential saving grace for Coach Daryl Royal whose teams performed markedly better once the Wishbone was in place. The Texas Wishbone offense culminated with the 1969 national championship. Daryl Royal became a UT icon while his program became one of the best in college football history. The Wishbone illustration shows similarities with the "Split T." The primary difference is the placement of the three backs in slightly different locations. A second difference from a personnel/formation perspective is the Wishbone features split ends rather than tight ends.

The "I" Formation

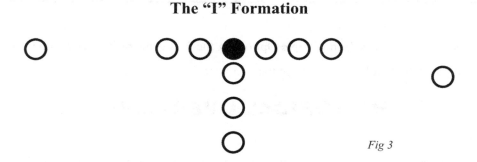

Fig 3

The "I" Formation (Figure 3) became the next prominent version of option football after the Wishbone. University of Nebraska running the "I" under Coach Tom Osborn in the 1980s and 1990s heavily influenced "Tex Bone" co-creator Tom Ross. During Osborne's tenure the "I" formation offense fueled their triple option to three national championships. Readers who study the Tex-Bone system in this book notice formation sets, play calls, strategies, personnel groupings, and other references that resemble those used at Nebraska under Coach Osborn.

The Flexbone

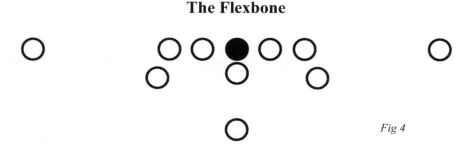

Fig 4

The Flexbone (Figure 4) serves the dual role of both a formation and as an offense when developed in detail. The Flexbone triple option offense is what most people think of when they envision modern option football. It is closely associated with coaches including Navy's Ken Niumatalolo and Paul Johnson at Georgia Tech as an adaption of the Wishbone offense. Different types of offenses across the country use the Flexbone formation. The formation is easily applied to diverse offensive needs because its not based on the triple option exclusively.

Spread Read Option (Double Option)

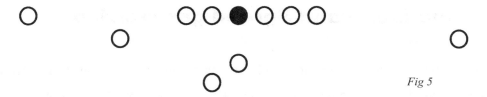

Fig 5

The spread read option (or double option) is equally noteworthy when examining the history of option football. Despite not being a true "triple option" attack, the system led to the creation of defensive schemes that in recent years inform how teams generally combat triple offense plays such as the outside veer. There are many notable coaches that ran spread read option (or zone read as it is popularly labeled). Two of those coaches were Bill Snyder at Kansas State in the 1990s and Urban Meyer at Utah in the early 2000s. Coaches in the years proceeding borrowed heavily from Snyder and Meyer in an attempt to mirror their successes.

It is important to note that the spread read option offense (Figure 5) is really a double option offense where the pitch phase is omitted. In double read option you start with the beginning phase of triple option—the "dive phase." The pitch phase is then eliminated when the "pitch man" is blocked. Pseudo triple option schemes of the past decade such as run-pass options (popularized as "RPO" on television broadcasts) were developed to reintroduce the pitch phase by creating a downfield pass option. Upon closer examination these spread read option offenses are deeply rooted in triple option football—regardless of what they are called or whether offensive coordinators want to admit it or not.

Spread Veer Triple Option

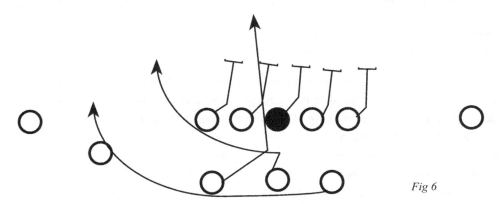

Fig 6

Triple option football is still alive in the college football landscape today—especially in the Service Academies (Army, Navy, and Air Force). Spread veer triple option (Figure 6) is a modern adaptation developed by former West Virginia Head Coach Rich Rodriguez in the 2000s. His primary-run scheme featured a hybrid veer and zone concept ran as a triple option that looked like a traditional outside veer. Rodriguez paired the hybrid with an open split-back spread formation that provided dive and pitch options. WVU also featured elements of modern spread football by operating from an open spread formation.

THE EVOLUTION OF THE TEX-BONE: how the Flexbone and Spread got married

Texas is a spread offense state. From high schools to colleges the offenses run wide open and fast. Defenses match the offenses with 4-2-5 cover 4 schemes in an attempt to match field width and deal with RPOs. It's a chess match that fuels some of the best football in the nation. Naturally there are outliers. At Southwestern University a new offense was born, the "Tex-Bone." Develop in tandem with Tom Ross; it is triple option for the 21st century. Our new system combines old-school Flexbone with a modern spread offense into one Texas-sized attack that leaves opponents scrambling to solve both the triple option and the spread at the same time.

Courtesy: Joe Austin

I was raised a spread coach. As an assistant offensive coordinator at Concordia University, St. Paul (MN) I helped shape an offense that finished 7th in the NCAA in total offense and 13th in scoring in 2002. The next year we finished 6th in total offense and 20th in scoring.

I began coordinating offenses at Augsburg College in 2004 before moving to the University of Dubuque in 2005. My year at Augsburg became my first experience working with Tom Ross.

At Dubuque, our offense became tops in the Iowa Intercollegiate Athletic Conference. Our achievements helped revitalize a Spartan program mired in two decades of losing seasons. In my first year (2005) the Spartans finished 20th in the NCAA in passing. By my last year at UD (2007) we placed 27th in the nation in both scoring offense and total offense and 29th in rushing offense. In 2019 our quarterback (Jermar Jackson) is being inducted into the University of Dubuque Athletic Hall of Fame.

In 2008, I became the head coach and offensive coordinator at Hanover College (Indiana). Serving as architects of another rebuild, our staff guided the Panthers to back-to-back second place finishes in the Heartland Intercollegiate Conference. My tenure at Hanover was highlighted by the performance of wide receiver Daniel

Courtesy: Marissa Austin

Passafiume who in 2009 set the all-time, all-divisions NCAA record for catches in a game with 25 against Franklin College. Two of our receivers won NCAA statistical championships for receptions: Tyler Thiems and Passafiume (#1 in the picture below). The Panthers finished 9th in the NCAA in passing offense in 2009. In my fourth year the Panthers finish 3rd in the nation in red zone offensive efficiency, 30th in passing offense and 35th in scoring offense.

Courtesy: Merry Ross

I was given the task of reintroducing football at Southwestern University in 2012. This became my greatest challenge as a coach thus far. Dubuque and Hanover were rebuild jobs—SU was a rebirth. Once a charter member of the Southwest Conference, the school dropped football in 1950 and didn't bring it back to the field until the fall of 2013.

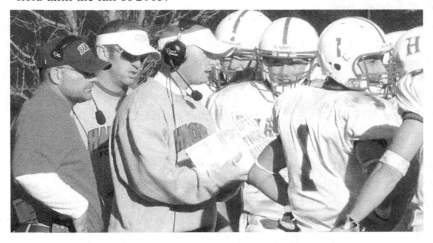

By 2016, we built the top offense in the Southern Collegiate Athletic Conference. The season culminated with a conference championship. I was humbled to receive Coach of the Year honors by my peers.

Tom Ross joined our staff in 2008 at Hanover College as the defensive coordinator. Coach Ross always provided excellent insights on offense at both Augsburg and Hanover even though his focus was on defense. Tom stayed on the defensive side until 2016 when the time was right for him to move to offense with me.

Tom was head coach of the Stuttgart Scorpions in the first division of the German Football League after our time together at Augsburg and prior to us reuniting at Hanover. Tom's Flexbone attack with the Scorpions was the equivalent of a Panzer tank—running roughshod over the south conference of the GFL and landing them in the German Bowl for the first time in team history. Tom was elected to the Scorpions Hall of Fame in 2016. He remains the most iconic coach in the history of the organization today.

Back to the evolution of the Tex-Bone…

Tom joined me on the offensive side in 2016. The original idea was to add Tom's Flexbone as an auxiliary offense to complement our spread. This hybrid system became the top offense in the SCAC,

powering us to a 6-0 conference record. At that point the Tex-Bone really didn't exist yet—the spread and option offense remained separate components used in different situations depending on the game plan.

Bryan Hicks, (our senior quarterback and a spread expert) didn't even practice the option. Don't feel bad for Bryan though (#14 below). The 2019 season marks his third year playing professionally. During this season he set the National Arena League all-time record for touchdown passes in a single game with nine. Our freshman understudy (Fred Hover) ran the option in 2016. The task of mastering the option and the spread was especially challenging and rewarding for Hover. Hover's year as a playing understudy became a key element in the emerging Tex-Bone system.

The idea of using a primary and auxiliary offense wasn't a new one for us. We did this previously at Augsburg College in 2004. Coach Ross (Associate Head Coach and Defensive Coordinator at the time) suggested to me that we add some Flexbone triple option to the team's repertoire for our last game of the season against St. Olaf College. We wanted to see how it looked and explore if it was something to carry forward into the future. The first triple option litmus test yielded 364 rushing yards (526 total yards) and 42 points. With that the seed was planted.

Though the experiment didn't continue into the next year (we both exited Augsburg College after the 2004 season), I carried the lessons learned about triple option to the University of Dubuque. As a way to help our rebuild at Dubuque I incorporated the Flexbone into several game plans for two seasons until our primary spread offense was running at breakneck speed. At that point triple option was relegated to the back page of the playbook—put into hibernation until 2016 when the marrying of the Flexbone and spread resumed.

The Tex-Bone was really born in 2017. Our plan at the time was to keep the primary and auxiliary offenses separate after the previous year's successes. There was one complicating factor with this decision: our new quarterback (Fred Hover) was able to adroitly run both offenses. We knew we needed to start developing ways to make everything congruent. This dual skilled luxury led to the organic evolution of game plans that included more and more triple option from traditional spread formations.

Courtesy: Chuck Pledge

Naturally there was still plenty of pure Flexbone and pure spread. Ultimately the hybrid elements—the 21st century triple option—became the big play catalyst. The results spoke for themselves as the Pirates finished 2nd in the nation in rushing and 9th in the nation in total offense in 2017. Defenses didn't know what was coming with different formations, different personnel, and different schemes. Was it a spread play? Was the triple option coming? It was hard to defend by design.

Over our first two years in the American Southwestern Conference we faced eleven opponents ranked in national polls, five play-off teams, three conference champions, and two national champions. To say we played good competition is a strong understatement. Against the best of what Division III offers we averaged 36 points per game with the Tex-Bone. In the process we posted our second and third consecutive winning seasons. The Tex-Bone is here to stay.

PHILOSOPHY: what is the Tex-Bone and how does it work?

The Tex-Bone is triple option for the 21st century. It combines triple option with spread concepts. The Tex-Bone allows teams to takes traditional option schemes and run them from nontraditional option alignments and formations.

Spread defenses are often predictable. Teams set defensive philosophies around how they align and handle the spread because spread formations are almost exclusively what defenses see in today's game. Defensive coordinators are prepared to line up against 2x1 Open, 2x2 Open, and 3x1 Open. They know how they prefer to line up against TE trips as well as H-Back formations. This predictability is an advantage for Tex-Bone triple option coaches.

Standing in direct contrast to the predictability of spread offenses is the unpredictability of the Tex-Bone. Every play is available in spread or option formations. Tex-Bone teams are less predictable in terms of formation tendencies than their spread counterparts. Every formation is an option look. Traditional option formations (such as our Shotgun Flexbone) are also home to a variety of non-option runs and passes. In aggregate the spread and option becomes a unified system with nearly innumerable variances.

A goal of the Tex-Bone is to eliminate predictability. Defensive coordinators look for predictability in personnel, down and distance, etc. Elements of predictability are reduced in the Tex-Bone. Aspects that coordinators typically look for become increasingly difficult to identify. Film study of the Tex-Bone is extremely difficult. Normal tendencies of cookie-cutter spread offenses are gone. Game planning against the Tex-Bone is now a complicated proposition.

The Tex-Bone provides modern advances to time-tested of schemes. They come in the form of minor adjustments such as operating from the shotgun for example. These modern advances create competitive advantages over standard spread offenses.

Old school limitations are gone. Starting in the shotgun means we do not motion our wingback pre-snap to get into pitch relationship. The play hits at a speed that allows the pitch player to start from a stationary position. Previous iterations of the triple option—particularly those that are ran from under center—hit at a speed that require the pitch back to motion toward the pitch relationship prior to the snap. Eliminating the need to motion the pitch player creates a tremendous advantage because the defense does not know which way the play is going.

Spread formations plays get a "free pass" when all of your opponent's prep time is spent on learning how to defend the triple option. When opponents design a defense for the Flexbone formation and adjust their base spread defense to cover the dive, quarterback, and pitch they gloss over game plan adjustments that change how spread formations are defended. This advantage flips the script by making spread the unaccounted-for element.

Because of this, Tex-Bone teams are likely to see a predictable defensive alignment when they line up in spread. This defensive predictability increases the likelihood of spread play success. Defensive preparations are a difficult task because the Tex-Bone is a triple option attack with a wide variety of formations and personnel groupings. Spread formation plays in the Tex-Bone gain an in-game advantage because the defensive game plan isn't geared towards defending them. Defenses often run a base defense when they see a spread formation because every defensive alignment must be sound versus triple option. The result is an instant advantage.

Teams put a high priority on run defense when preparing for the Tex-Bone. They are forced to put an extra emphasis on who covers the dive, the quarterback, and the pitch specifically. Defenses are forced to combat the triple threat for every formation they potentially see (and there are many). Opponents often get lost in the details of three responsibilities for each play in multiple formations—moving play action pass coverage to the back burner. This is an offensive advantage come game day.

Disguised looks are an additional advantage at the line of scrimmage. Lining up "properly" against the Tex-Bone doesn't necessarily mean the defense will get the desired result. Runs and passes look identical in the Tex-Bone. Opponents do not know what is coming until it happens. The deception makes play action pass opportunities plentiful. All Tex-Bone plays—no matter if it's a run or a pass—look identical through the mesh of the quarterback and fullback. Runs and passes look identical even longer depending on the play. Plays that begin with the same appearance greatly enhance the ability to execute play action.

Why the Tex-Bone?

The uniqueness of the Tex-Bone makes it difficult to defend because running triple option from spread formations is a fairly unique approach. Defenses are tasked with stopping both spread formations and the Shotgun Flexbone. Advantages are multiplied when opponents lack experience against the Flexbone. Individualized game plans for Tex-Bone teams from school-to-school and week-to-week assure that even if an opponent sees the Flexbone before they are still guessing come game day. This inexperience is an additional challenge for the opponent and an additional opportunity for you.

The Tex-Bone is the first triple option system that uses the Power Run as the foundation play. Even defensive coaches that are adept at stopping the option are forced to pay close attention to the Power Run orientation of the Tex-Bone.

The Tex-Bone gives teams the opportunity to play against predictable defensive alignments. When Tex-Bone teams line up in a spread formation they are likely to see the opponent's base spread defense. Every defense knows how they like to defend spread formations. In preparation they are likely to use this familiarity as the base of their game plan against the Tex-Bone. Some variations are likely to occur. Because opponents emphasize triple option readiness those defensive adjustments are most likely basic variations of their base defense.

The Tex-Bone builds in defensive disincentives. Option football (of any variety) builds in line game and blitz dissuasion. The speed of play, run-pass deception, multiple pre-snap looks, and triple responsibilities in the Tex-Bone discourages the use of twists, stunts, or blitzes. Putting option plays in a team's arsenal naturally limits the likelihood of seeing line games or blitzes as a regular in-game defensive tactic.

The Tex-Bone provides two offenses with one set of players—successfully combining the triple option with modern spread offenses. This combination allows teams to become more diverse and complex with the same number of players.

The triple option system works with your personnel—to a certain extent. Many coaches subscribe to the pre-conceived notion of "Run option if you lack talent". There are two reasons I believe coaches feel this way.

1. Teams avoid blocking players by optioning them. Physically not blocking players is an advantage when a team is physically outmatched.
2. Option teams with superior execution are sometimes able to beat teams with superior talent. Coaches begin to assume option football is a magical solution after witnessing it firsthand.

The reality is option football bolsters your personnel. What needs remembering is that teams with inferior personnel struggle against exceptional opponents regardless of the offense implemented. Option football isn't a quick fix and the Tex-Bone isn't a magic bullet for overmatched teams. The year before this book was written we played the eventual national champion. They made us look bad. The triple option was unable to overcome an immensely talented opponent in that situation. Conference champion and national champion teams are made up of eleven talented players on each side of the ball. While the triple option allows teams the luxury of not blocking two defenders it still means the other nine must be dealt with.

Option football teams need talented athletes at quarterback and wing/slot positions to function effectively. Teams that lack players with the ability to move the ball downfield often struggle against equal or greater opponents over the course of the season. Finding the right personnel for the offense (or creating the right offense for the personnel) is the primary responsibility of a coach or offensive coordinator.

The only limit to the Tex-Bone is coaching imagination. Later in this chapter we present twelve different ways our team executes triple option from the Tex-Bone. The list we provide is in no way exhaustive. We used many additional alignments over the last two seasons to supplement the twelve we illustrate.

The Tex-Bone offers an advantage in game planning because the Flexbone is hard to predict. Teams see an opponent's game plan-specific defense against the Flexbone. The reason it gets game planned is the Flexbone is not part of most team's base defensive package. Few teams see the Flexbone and triple option during the course of a season. They are particularly unlikely to see a Power-based Shotgun Flexbone triple option scheme. An opponent needs to see two Tex-Bone teams on the schedule to enter a game prepared to defend the Shotgun Flexbone triple option. This is highly unlikely given the newness and uniqueness of the offense.

Spread-based defenses generally do not scheme to combat the Flexbone before game week. Because of this factor a Tex-Bone/Flexbone team is able to present something unique on game day that was not previously seen on film. Defensive inexperience with the Flexbone is an advantage when leveraged properly. A team's own familiarity with executing the Flexbone outweighs the potential disadvantage of not seeing how a defense plans to defend before game day. In this case the proactive advantage is gained from the Flexbone making opponents react to what they see. The difference is best explained as the Flexbone makes defense respond to it instead of the Flexbone responding to the defense.

Spread defenses are fairly easy to predict (this idea was mentioned previously). This is another advantage. Even if a team sees a different than expected spread defense on game day it doesn't matter because Tex-Bone schemes are rules based. The rules of the Tex-Bone let teams run Flexbone and spread formations regardless of defensive alignments and strategies.

The Tex-Bone features an economy of techniques from a player perspective. What this means is the offense does not require a large set of individual skills for different positions. This reduction of specialized skills is advantageous. Skills are broken into components that are easily digested by players new to the system. Practicing those component skills in detailed, strategic repetition allows players to develop better Tex-Bone specific skills in a shorter amount of time. Players are then able to move from the learning to execution stage of the offense more quickly. This economy of technique puts athletes in a better position to react and play faster. This is especially important when considering the skill level of opponents. It is a distinct disadvantage at the college level when players end up slowing down because they are unsure about their assignment. The Tex-Bone helps remediate this concern.

We break our positions into smaller subgroups for specialized training whenever possible. We split our inside and outside receivers into two smaller groups for example. It makes sense to differentiate the positions and focus specifically on their required skills given that their responsibilities are different.

Offensive line demands are similar to those of skill position groups. We do not expect our linemen to execute a multitude of blocks. Our footwork is simplified in a manner that allows us to let our athletes focus on aggressive, physical play. The net result is we present an opponent with the appearance of doing a lot without overburdening our linemen with too many individual skills.

Why Coaches May Not Like the Tex-Bone

A fair overview of the Tex-Bone requires an examination of the offense in a manner that invites skepticism. This skepticism is healthy and welcome. It helps answer questions about the system and leads to further innovations that keep the Tex-Bone successful.

Double teams are deemphasized in the Tex-Bone system. On most schemes the intent is to create displacement horizontally along the line of scrimmage rather than vertically. If a team is committed to double teams—particularly on Power—this system potentially yields limited results. Step together double teams in the Tex-Bone that move the line of scrimmage vertically are not a primary blocking technique. Horizontal movement in triple option is important because it opens lanes for dive backs and quarterback inserts. Double teams tend to limit or slow the opening of lanes. Because of this risk the double team is not used in the Tex-Bone.

Versatile wing and slot players in the Tex-Bone are a must. These are the players a Tex-Bone team relies on heavily whether it's an option pitch or a forward pass. Tex-Bone teams must also possess an instinctual, intelligent triggerman at quarterback. This does not mean a team needs a 1,000-yard quarterback rusher. What it does mean is that at team needs a quarterback that effectively distributes the football by making quality dive and pitch reads. To maintain effectiveness the quarterback must make a few simple checks in various situations and react to the defense as the play unfolds.

Shotgun vs. Under Center

The Tex-Bone operates from the shotgun for everything we do. There are certain advantages to this. As mentioned before, a key advantage is eliminating pitch back motion before the play. Pre-snap motion by the pitch player is a limiting factor for other option systems as the pre-snap motion tips off where the ball is going. The ability to create misdirection is now enhanced with the offense in control of when to motion and when not motion before the play. Operating from the shotgun also increases the number of possible pitch players and formations.

The tradeoff accompanying this advantage is that option schemes such as midline or freeze option become difficult to execute. It is difficult to read the 3-technique when operating from the shotgun because the play does not hit fast enough. Loss of effectiveness for these schemes are a clear limitation.

The Shotgun QB Sneak

The Shotgun QB sneak is probably my favorite play in all of football. Running out of shotgun makes the quarterback sneak an essential, advantageous component of our offense. Working downhill by running through the snap lets the quarterback gain a bigger head of steam than if he starts from under center. This momentum leads to sizeable gains by putting the defense on its heels from the time the play starts. This quick start also gives the quarterback better vision for the play as its unfolding—seeing where to insert himself into the line of scrimmage on the designed run.

When running quarterback sneak from the shotgun we produce touchdowns from plays that hit as wide as the C-gap. Lining up in shotgun gives the quarterback better vision before the snap as well—allowing him to adjust when defenses pinch in anticipation of the run. Adopting this play is something for all shotgun teams to consider.

CH 2: FORMATION FAMILIES & PERSONNEL

FORMATION FAMILIES

The Tex-Bone is based on four basic formation families:

1.   The Shotgun Flexbone (available with or without a tight end)
2.   The Empty Flexbone (available with or without a tight end)
3.   2x1 Open with a wing (aligned to the strong or weak side of the formation)
4.   Spread family of formations: 2x2, 3x1 (both open or with a tight end)

Other empty spread formations are also used (3x2 and 4x1) in the Tex-Bone. Most of the spread empty formations we use are game plan specific. These spread empty formations are considered cousin to the 2x2 and 3x1 formation family.

Figure 7 shows base Shotgun Flexbone. There are multiple ways to run the Flexbone with different personnel from this standard set. The basic personnel grouping in Shotgun Flexbone includes two running backs at wing, a fullback behind the quarterback, and two split ends. Players are referred to as wings when their alignment splits the outside leg of the tackle. When players move to a slot position there are no changes in their assignment. The Shotgun Flexbone is discussed again several times throughout the rest of the book.

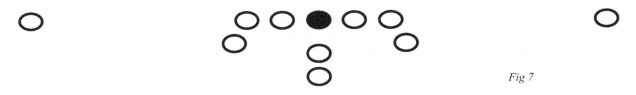

Fig 7

As mentioned before, we play from the Flexbone with three running backs (two running backs in the wing position and one running back as a fullback behind the quarterback) as shown in Figure 8. This is not the only personnel choice however.

RB   RB

Fig 8

We also play from this formation with four wide receivers. This allows us to put two wide receivers as wings and two wide receivers as the split ends (see Figure 9).

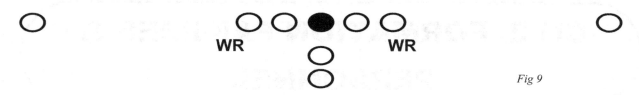

WR   **WR**

Fig 9

We also run a combination of personnel with one running back at wing and one wide receiver at wing. Figure 10 shows of one receiver and one running back at wing.

WR   **RB**

Fig 10

We also create a personnel group that inserts an extra running back as a split receiver (as shown in Figure 11).

RB

Fig 11

The key is using your personnel to do the things they are best at. When considering player strengths as a qualifying factor for constructing personnel groupings you instantly notice the new luxury the Tex-Bone provides in terms of building a wide variety of personnel groupings.

The Empty Flexbone (see Figure 12) is another formation the Tex-Bone uses frequently. Personnel in the Empty Flexbone are amendable—just like the Shotgun Flexbone. We are also able to run this formation with or without a tight end. A coach is able to put running backs or wide receivers at both wing positions. An additional option is to deploy one receiver and one running back at the wings. What a coach chooses depends on the play call and players designated as best suited to execute the play.

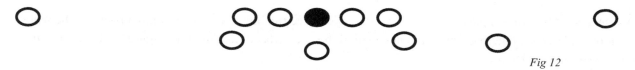

Fig 12

The 2x1 Open formation (in this case with a wing to the weak side in Figure 13) is the first example of a spread formation in the Tex-Bone. The basic way to run this formation is with two running backs (one as the fullback behind the quarterback and one running back at the wing position) with three receivers (two as split ends and one at slot receiver).

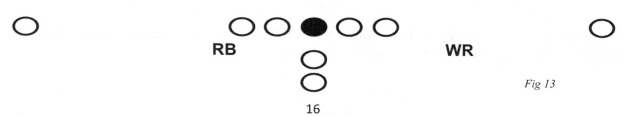

RB   **WR**

Fig 13

There are other options as to how you can run this formation however. 2x1 Open is also available with a three running back look in Figure 14.

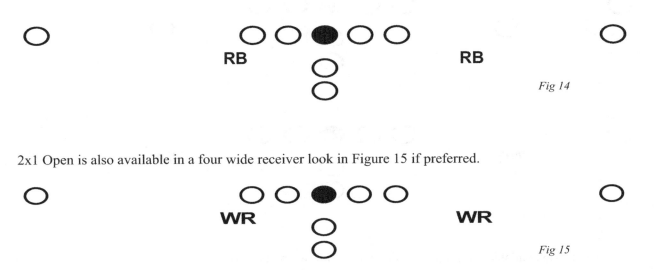

Fig 14

2x1 Open is also available in a four wide receiver look in Figure 15 if preferred.

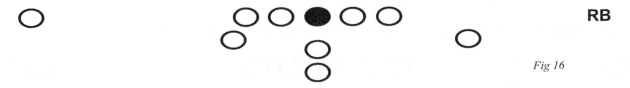

Fig 15

Mix-and-matching running backs and wide receivers are easily done from both looks.

A final option places an additional running back as a split wide receiver (Figure 16 creates the potential for four running backs on the field).

RB

Fig 16

The key is to utilize personnel in their best positions based on ability and the requirements of your plays.

We are also able to run 2x1 Open with a wing to the strong side as in Figure 17. 2x1 Open with a wing maintains the same versatility as standard 2x1 Open in terms of the number of running backs and wide receivers available for specific plays or needs. We make decisions regarding where we want to deploy our personnel as the offense is installed at the beginning of the season and again as game plans are implemented from week-to-week.

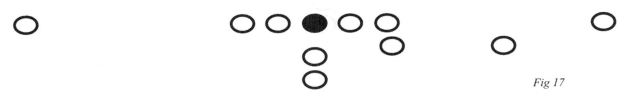

Fig 17

The 2x2 Open formation (shown in Figure 18) demonstrates the same versatility. The basic way to do this is with four wide receivers and one running back in the backfield (see Figure 19).

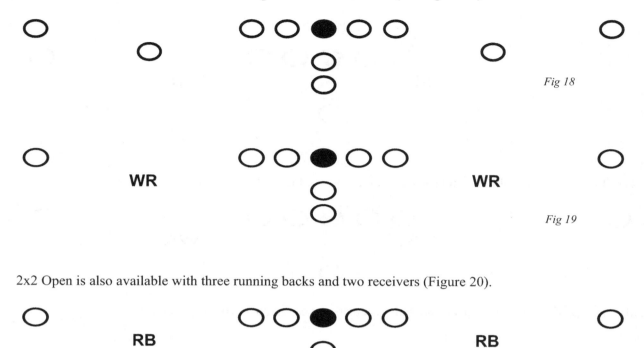

Fig 18

WR   WR

Fig 19

2x2 Open is also available with three running backs and two receivers (Figure 20).

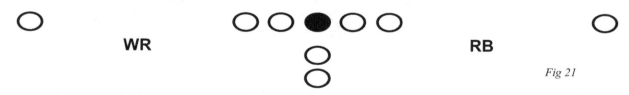

RB   RB

Fig 20

Figure 21 shows how 2x2 Open looks with three wide receivers and two running backs.

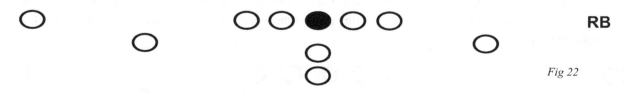

WR   RB

Fig 21

Figure 22 shows how 2x2 Open looks with an additional running back at the split receiver position.

RB

Fig 22

A 2x2 Tight set provides the same opportunities to mix and match personnel. Figure 23 shows that a running back or a wide receiver is able to line up in the slot. A receiver or running back is also able to line up at the flanker position.

Fig 23

The versatility continues with the 3x1 Open set shown in Figure 24. The base look for 3x1 Open is with four wide receivers and one running back. But the possibilities do not end there. The 3x1 Open is also available with three running backs and two receivers. Coaches are best served to set their personnel based on individual needs.

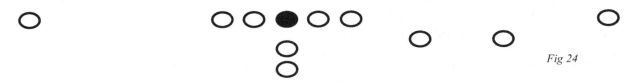

Fig 24

The same thing is true with the 3x1 Tight set in Figure 25. 3x1 Tight features three running backs and one wide receiver or three wide receivers and one running back. Teams are also able to run the set with two wide receivers and two running backs.

Fig 25

Coach's note: while a "Pistol" alignment is the Tex-Bone default, we will frequently off-set the running back to run dives and plays such as Power Read.

PERSONNEL

Let's discuss personnel in greater detail. The discussion of formations on previous pages highlight the flexibility the Tex-Bone offense creates in terms of personnel deployment. The following are some additional considerations regarding personnel.

Wing/slot combinations are ideal. Players that are able to line up at both wing and slot are extremely useful. Players like this eliminate substitutions based on formation. It also makes run and pass plays seamless in terms of appearance (setting up play action) and reduces predictability based on personnel grouping.

It is important to remember that the job of the wing and slot player is identical in the Tex-Bone. There is no change in assignment—run or pass—based on a wing or slot alignment. Schematically they are the same position. This does not mean that their roles are always executed the same however. There are differences in roles and responsibilities between the wing and slot alignment. For this reason players that execute efficiently from both positions are diamonds.

Just because wings and slots are schematically the same doesn't diminish the advantage of taking a wing and moving him out to slot. The advantage lies in the change of formation from an option to spread look. When moving to a spread formation defenses then line up in familiar sets that are more easily exploitable.

Substituting and specializing is strongly suggested. Offenses are well served to use players in roles that fit their skill set and then substitute them out of roles that do not fit their skills. The Tex-Bone is no different. If a player is excellent at receiving the pitch but less adroit at other aspects of the offense it is advisable to just use them on the pitch exclusively until more skills develop.

Multiple personal options for the same formation are a defensive headache. Accentuate the positive and eliminate the negative. Ask players to do what they are good at even within the same formation. Do not ask them to do things they are not good at. This doesn't mean that player skill development is less critical—this simply means you don't pick the fruit until it is ripe.

CH 3: TEMPO, BACKFIELDS & FULLBACKS

TEMPO: pace of play

The Tex-Bone executes plays from any tempo. When considering the Tex-Bone it is important to understand that if you really like what you are currently doing with your offense in terms of tempo there is no reason to change from the current pace of play.

Huddle

Huddle pace is the first tempo installed in the Tex-Bone. Our team frequently huddles during the course of a game. Huddling is **not** done to slow the game down. We huddle to make sure the right personnel are on the field and that communication is reliable. Our huddle is done as crisply as possible. There are no prescribed spots in the huddle—there is no diagram telling players where to stand. The idea is to get close enough to the quarterback to hear the call and get lined up quickly. Slot/wing players and split ends learn how far from the offensive line group to stand and still get the call. Players also learn to echo the call to each other.

An efficient huddle is often faster than other alternatives by comparison. Consider a no huddle offense where everyone looks to the sideline to get nonverbal communication from cards or signals for example. It takes time for everyone to get the call, lineup in the formation, and run the play. Our operational speed is generally not slower than a traditional no huddle pace because we change personnel quickly, make the huddle call, and run out of the huddle to get set. When players are familiar with the system the speed increases.

Huddle Check

In some game plans we use particular formations, plays, or personnel groups labeled as "huddle indicators." Hearing one of these indicators means we huddle prior to executing the next play. Some weeks the huddle check is not used at all and some weeks it is used a lot. This tempo means we huddle for some plays and not huddle for others.

The reason we designate something as a huddle indicator is game specific with the goal of avoiding tendencies that other teams pick up on. We do not huddle just because we're going to run an option play or because we're going to run a play with a long name. The specific aspects of each game plan that indicate a huddle check are unique from game-to-game.

The overarching intent is to create an advantage that is exploited with our pre-play tempo. We huddle when it is advantageous to our offense. We do not huddle when we find the different pace equally advantageous.

No Huddle

The Tex-Bone also runs effectively as a no huddle offense. There is a multitude of ways to signal or send plays to quarterback and offensive personnel. Any no huddle communication system a coach is familiar with and prefers to use is suitable for executing the Tex-Bone as a no huddle offense.

Hurry

The fourth tempo is a hurry tempo. All teams need a hurry-up tempo. Triple option teams are not exempt from this requirement. Teams needs to familiarize themselves with all of the strategies associated with increased speed to use hurry up effectively. Homer Smith wrote the definitive philosophy on how to execute the hurry up offense in my opinion. He recommended that split ends, slots, and wings do not flip sides of the field from play-to-play. If a receiver gets caught downfield on our sideline they simply run off and someone substitutes in for the next play. With practice the Tex-Bone is an excellent hurry up offense operating as efficiently as any other system.

BACKFIELD ACTIONS:
12 ways the Tex-Bone is used to run and pass

The following pages detail twelve ways to execute the triple option Tex-Bone offense. Examining how the Tex-Bone runs and passes the ball gives coaches an idea of its versatility. These illustrations do not represent all of our Tex-Bone triple option formations. Twelve were selected because it's a round number and because they represent a strong cross section of possibilities without overburdening the reader. All twelve examples show dive option action to the right. Each formation is calibrated to show this.

The formation in Figure 26 is the Shotgun Flexbone. It is a good starting place because it represents the basic way to run triple option.

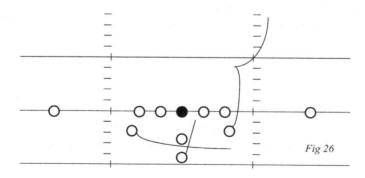

Fig 26

Figure 27 shows the right wing moved out to a slot position. Moving the wing changes the formation from a traditional Flexbone option into a 2x1 Open spread. This changes the defensive philosophy from "how do we cover the Flexbone" to "how do we cover 2x1 Open spread?" Every defense creates a 2x1 Open philosophy. Opponents are likely to defend this formation with a look that is standard to their defense. Figure 27 shows a dive towards the open slot.

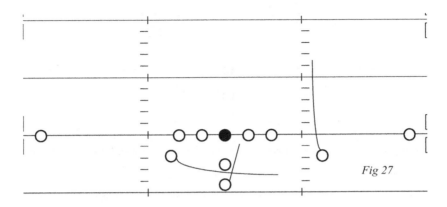

Fig 27

Figure 28 shows the dive option towards the wing from 2x1 Open spread.

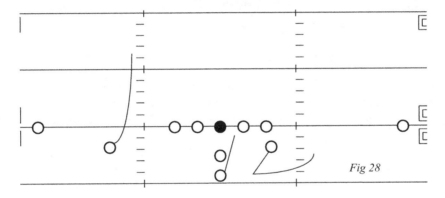

Fig 28

The next Figure (29) shows how to move the slot back to a wing position—essentially motioning to a modified Flexbone before running dive option towards the side where the motion originated. At least fifty percent of the time we run dive option away from the direction that the motion originated. Schematically this demonstrates a sort of counter influence.

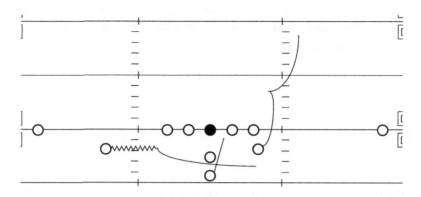

Figure 30 shows motion down to a wing position in a 2x2 Open set. Essentially this creates a modified 2x1 Open formation.

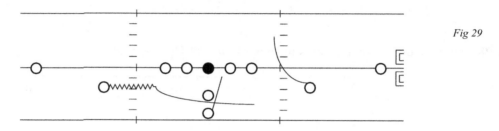

Fig 29

Another way to run dive option out of 2x2 Open is to motion a slot down to a wing and then run option back in the direction the motion player started (see Figure 31). Running option toward the motion is an effective tendency breaker and counter maneuver when defenses shift in response to motion.

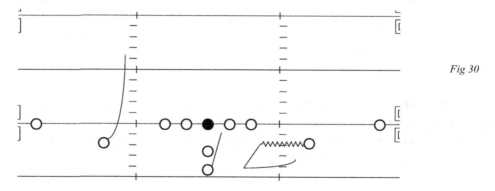

Fig 30

Figure 32 shows open slot motion to a wing with the option running toward the motion side. This motion shifts the play into a modified Flexbone formation. A key component of motioning to Flexbone rather than lining up in Flexbone is it traps the defense into a spread philosophy instead of a Flexbone philosophy.

Fig 31

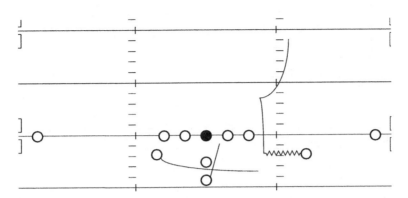

We are also able to align the wing to the strong side of the formation—the same side of the 2x1 formation where the slot is (see Figure 33). This allows us to run dive option towards the alignment wing.

Fig 32

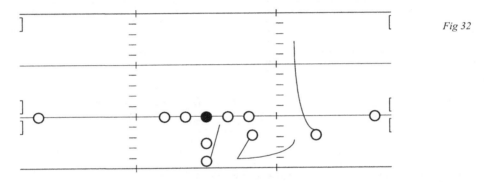

Figure 34 shows motion by the strong side wing to the weak side. The wing moves back toward the open slot at the snap to run option.

Fig 33

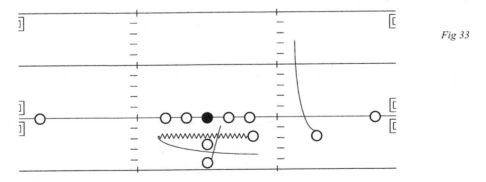

Another variation is running option away from the strong side wing. The option is away from the wing's initial alignment in Figure 35.

Fig 34

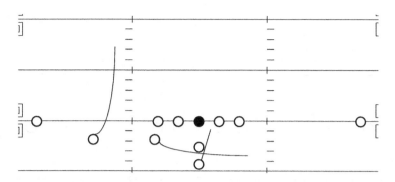

A 2x2 Open bunch formation is shown in Figure 36. The advantage of the bunch formation is that a slot receiver doesn't need a large head start to get into proper pitch relationship.

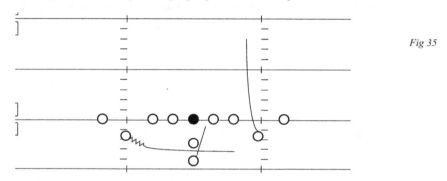

Fig 35

The 3x1 Open in Figure 37 motions a slot receiver down into a wing position. Generally the slot is moved over the top of the quarterback to run option toward the split end when we run this play. This is not our only choice for running the play however. An additional choice is bringing the motion player back in the direction he started from.

Fig 36

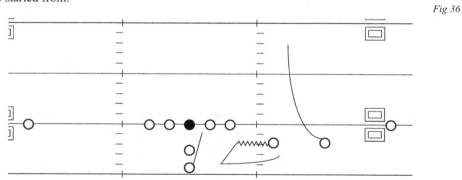

Fig 37

FULLBACK PATHS

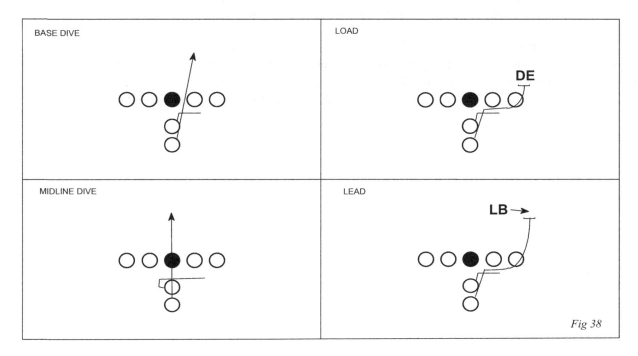

Fig 38

Base Dive

Fullback paths are the same for run and pass plays. The base fullback path is shown in the upper left of Figure 38. The fullback is aiming at the A-gap. The quarterback's footwork matches the path of the fullback as they both step toward the line of scrimmage.   Additional details about the fullback/quarterback mesh are outlined later.

Fullback Load

The term "load" by definition is assigning the fullback to block the defensive end (top right of Figure 38). The load path begins the same as the dive path. All four of our dive paths look identical through the mesh. After meshing with the quarterback the fullback veers his path to the edge and blocks the defensive end.

Fullback Lead

The bottom right of Figure 38 shows fullback lead. "Lead" is defined as assigning the fullback to the play side linebacker. Fullbacks take the same A-Gap aiming point on all dives. After meshing the fullback works to the outside and blocks the linebacker.

Midline Dive

The bottom left of Figure 38 shows the midline dive. This is one of our back pocket choices used in specific option situations when needed. We also use this choice for one-back spread runs. The advantage of the midline dive is it accounts for defensive ends that are difficult for the quarterback to read.

Some defensive ends try to slow play the dive mesh. What this means is the defensive end gives the quarterback a look that entices the dive handoff before collapsing on the fullback after the exchange. Another slow play tactic is to sit at the line of scrimmage and wait to see where the ball is going before reacting. Moving the dive line inside and diving down the midline forces the defensive end to commit faster.

CH 4: NUMBERING SYSTEM

This chapter will look at a sample Tex-Bone numbering system. Let's begin by stating that there is nothing magical about the Tex-Bone numbering system we use. A team that already runs some of the Tex-Bone schemes and has a naming or numbering system they like is able to continue doing so while developing additional terminology as needed.

The *first number* (Figure 39) identifies whether the play goes to the right or the left in the Tex-Bone. The play is going to the right if the first number is even. The play is going to the left if the first number is odd. The first number also tells the play-side blockers what type of blocking scheme they execute. The *second number* tells backside blockers what blocking scheme they execute. Everyone needs to listen to the first number to know whether they are on the front side or backside of the play.

First Number

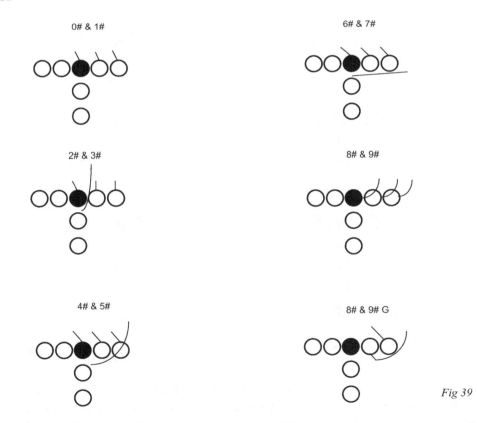

Fig 39

A first number of zero or one indicates an outside veer. Zero (treated as an even number) indicates a play going to the right as shown in Figure 39 (top left). A first number of one indicates a play running to the left. Two or three signifies an Iso scheme. An Iso consists of man-to-man blocking with an Isolation block coming through the open gap. Both two and three schemes are included in Figure 39 (middle left).

Four or five indicates power (bottom left of Figure 39). Veer and power are different even though they look alike. In veer the uncovered lineman works to the play-side linebacker. On power they uncovered lineman works to the backside linebacker. Power starts with front-side down blocks that lead to the backside linebacker. The Outside Veer (zero and one) and Power (four and five) look the same when taken at face value. For coaches new to the Tex-Bone the differences become easier to understand the more you study the offense.

A six or seven (top right of Figure 39) indicates power blocking with a trap coming from the backside.

Eight or nine in the Tex-Bone (center right of Figure 39) features reach and overtake blocking (otherwise known as full scoop blocking) typically found in speed option plays.

Coaches are able to make tags to any numbered play. The bottom right of Figure 39 shows an "eight" indicating an outside zone scheme to the right. A "G" is also tagged—indicating a tackle and guard fold used in the G Load Option play.

Second Number

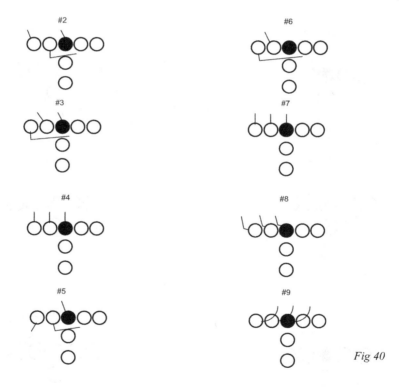

Fig 40

A second number of two (top left column of Figure 40) indicates a guard pull to block the play-side linebacker. This is an isolation block done by a guard. The center and backside tackle know what they need to do because they know the guard is pulling to the front-side of the play. During the play the center back blocks and the tackle inside-out blocks the defensive end.

The tackle pulls to the front side linebacker if the second number is a three (left column of Figure 40). Three is a Tackle Iso similar to how a two is a Guard Iso. The center and the guard know what to do because a three call indicates a tackle pull. The center covers the backside A-gap to the backside linebacker while the guard covers the backside B-gap to the backside linebacker. The guard picks up defensive ends that squeeze in.

A four (left column of Figure 40) indicates man-to-man base blocking. There is a gap responsible blocker for each gap responsible defender.

A five (bottom left column of Figure 40) tells the backside guard to pull and trap off the play side edge. A five also tells the front and backside linemen that this is a pass protection. Linemen know to push everything down at level one (line of scrimmage) rather than work to level two (linebackers). (Remember: linemen blocking downfield beyond three yards is a penalty.) Run-pass option coaches are not always concerned with illegal man downfield violations. Tex-Bone coaches need to display discretion in this area however. The center and tackle block aggressively—making sure they stay on level one.

A six (top right column of Figure 40) tells the tackle to pull and trap off the edge. On a six the center and guard block similar to a five—making sure they stay on the line of scrimmage.

A seven (right column of Figure 40 signifies the same responsibilities as a four only in this case the play is a pass. This does not mean players pass set however. They aggressively run block at the line of scrimmage. Linemen without a gap threat then work down to the next inside or outside threat. The seven call reminds linemen to not block downfield illegally.

An eight (right column of Figure 40) indicates gap blocking on the backside and a nine (bottom right column of Figure 40) is reach and overtake (or full scoop) outside blocking.

Summary: The first and second number combination in the Tex-Bone signifies a specific blocking scheme. We prefer two number designations because of the specific information it provides players. Single number or single-word designations require greater amounts of memorization for players. It also increases the likelihood of player confusion and missed in-play blocking assignments.

Just because we do not prefer single number calls doesn't mean it isn't advisable. The beginning of this chapter recommended using terminology and labels your team is already familiar with. Use the Tex-Bone double number system if it works best for you. Use another system if it is more beneficial. Tex-Bone play labels are logical and easy-to-understand by design. From a practice and execution perspective this is extremely advantageous.

THE FULL PLAY CALL

The next step is to combine the first number and second number to make a full play call. Detailed descriptions of all Tex-Bone schemes are later in the book.

Our base play (Power) is numbered 42 or 52 (Figure 41). The front side is a four if the play is going right or a five if the play is going left. The two denotes the blocking scheme to the backside of the play. The front side linemen backblock to the backside linebacker and the backside guard pulls to isolates the play-side linebacker. The center knows to backblock the first head up defender and the tackle blocks inside-out on the defensive end. These two numbers create a full power-blocking scheme for your offensive line. Coaches are able to add individualized aspects such as a tag to indicate a double pull power play. This Power concept is revisited later in the book.

42 Power (frontside 4, back side 2)

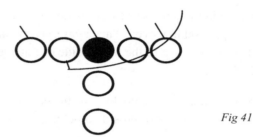

Fig 41

Tags can be added for thing like double pull

Another example is the Veer play in Figure 42. We call this a four. Coaches are able to call it a zero-four if desired. Players realize after a few practices that the play is really a front side zero with a backside four. The front side zero signifies gap blocking with a guard and tackle working to the play side linebacker. A backside four (3-for 3-blocking) accompanies this front side scheme.

04 Veer (frontside 0, backside 4)

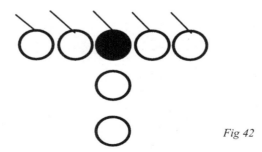

Fig 42

Speed option in Figure 43 is numbered an 89 (a front side eight and a backside nine). In Tex-Bone this is a speed option where the contain player becomes the option man. This scheme is also detailed in later chapters.

89 Speed (frontside 8, backside 9)

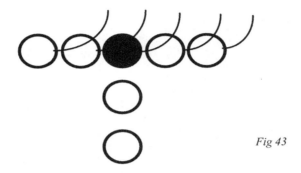

Fig 43

G Load is another base play for us (Figure 44). The example below is an 84 (the front side executes an eight and the backside executes a four). The front side eight includes a "G" tag that tells the guard and tackle to fold.

84 G (frontside 8, backside 4, G tag)

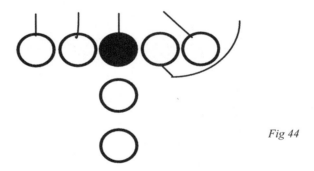

Fig 44

RUN GAME

5. Power Option

6. G Load Option

7. Double Pull Power

8. Speed Option

9. Power Read

10. Veer Option

11. Isos & Counters

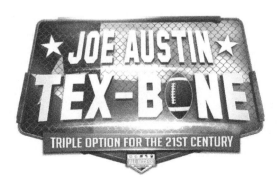

CH 5: POWER OPTION

POWER OPTION: the foundational play
in the Tex-Bone

The Tex-Bone is the first option system to feature Power run as its primary scheme.

Power was first introduced at the University of Michigan by head coach Fielding Yost in 1905. Yost won 16 national championships during his tenure at Michigan. Between 1901 and 1905 his "point a minute" squads outscored opponents 2821 to 40 while posting a 55-1 record.

The Basic Power Play

The basic Power play uses two lead blockers—typically the backside guard and fullback. The front side of the play uses down blocks working through to the backside linebacker. Multiple permutations of this play include Counter Trey, H-Back Counter and Power Read.

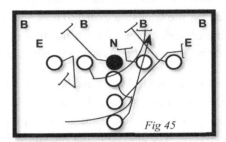

Fig 45

Figure 45 shows an "I" Formation Power play.

Tex-Bone Power Option

Tex-Bone Power is the cornerstone of the 21st century triple option. Using Power as the base of the Tex-Bone offers several benefits detailed throughout the chapter.

Power creates horizontal and vertical defensive displacement first and foremost. Some Power teams rely on vertical displacement via double teams on defensive tackles to open space for the ball carrier. Other Power systems (the Tex-Bone specifically) use horizontal stretch to open running lanes.

The rationale for grounding the Tex-Bone in a foundation of Power football is rooted in two distinct advantages. First, there is never a need to "check" out of Power. A coach calls Power and is able to run it. Power is a rule based play. Offensive players aren't thrown off by concerns over blocking assignments when the defensive front changes. If players are well versed in the rules of the play they know what the appropriate response to any changing alignment is. Slanting alignments, twisting line schemes, etc. are not difficult to deal with.

Second, Power Option easily pairs with play-action passes. Play-action from Power is something that most coaches are likely aware of already. Power Pass (a play-action three level flood) is nearly a century old. Teams potentially know this play as "Spider 2, Y-Banana" or another variation of the name.

Figure 46 details Tex-Bone Power Option against two fronts. Our analysis begins with the play side tackle. The play side tackle is the B-gap player. His assignment is to block any player aligned in his gap or any player that loops or blitzes to his gap. The play side tackle works to the backside linebacker if a defender does not appear in the gap.

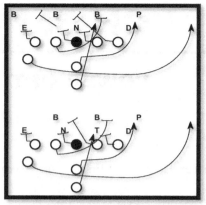

The play side guard is then the A-gap player. Like the tackle, his assignment is to block any player aligned in the A-gap or any other defender that loops or blitzes to his gap (similar assignment rules to the play side tackle). The play side guard also works to the backside linebacker if a defender does not appear in the gap. Combined the guard and tackle usually account for the playside defensive tackle and backside linebacker.

Fig 46

The center always back blocks the first player nearest him in Power. This backblock covers the space needed for the backside guard to pull and isolation block the play side linebacker. The pulling guard enters the line of scrimmage through the first open gap he finds. The pulling guard then works inside-out to the outside number of the play side linebacker (reach block).

The backside tackle works inside-out to block the defensive end. Figure 46 shows the tackle base blocking the defensive end. A backside tackle is also able to use a hinge block to reach the same result. Our block choice depends on the team we are playing and how they respond to the presentation of each block respectively. We also consider the strength of defensive personnel during the game planning process when deciding on a base or hinge technique. If the pulling guard is covered by a defensive tackle we will likely choose to hinge as this will aid the center with his back block.

The fullback is aligned behind the quarterback in the Power diagram (Figure 46). Our Power option dives the fullback to the A-gap (explained in greater depth later in the chapter). The wing is the pitch player. His alignment straddles the outside leg of the offensive tackle. The quarterback then reads the dive key first and the pitch key second. The dive key is the defensive end and the pitch key is the first linebacker outside of the box.

Power Option vs. Blitz

Nothing really changes when Power Options is ran against a blitz. Figure 47 shows Power Option against
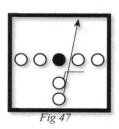
edge blitzes. The pitch key (shown as blitzing off of the edge) will be responsible for the pitch player or the quarterback. The quarterback can then identify the defensive end (dive key) as responsible for covering the dive on the inside. An offense knows if the pitch key is taking the pitch or the quarterback based on what the defense does with their safeties. (In most cases the blitzing pitch player takes the pitch and the safety takes the quarterback.)

Fig 47

Nothing changes for the offense from a schematic standpoint when the defense blitzes either. The play side tackle takes the B-gap to the backside linebacker. The play side guard blocks the A-gap to the backside linebacker.

All defensive linemen along with the backside linebacker are picked up in the Power Option blocking scheme. The center always back blocks the first player he encounters. The backside guard pulls for the play side linebacker and the backside tackle blocks inside-out man-to-man on the defensive end.

The fullback still runs the dive, the wing is still the pitch player, and the quarterback still reads the dive key to the pitch key against the blitz in Power Option. It is reasonable for the quarterback to anticipate that the dive key is taking the dive away. The quarterback is also able to expect that the blitzing pitch key is going to take away the wing. This defensive shift leaves the quarterback with the ball in a position to attack the vacated alley.

Remember, these are tendencies—not 100 percent guarantees. The quarterback must still react to what is seen even when a blitz is identified pre-snap. It is critical for the quarterback to avoid predetermining his decision based on the pre-snap read in any option play. Doing so potentially negates an advantage for big gains that develop mid-play.

FULLBACK FUNDAMENTALS

Base Dive

The fullback path leads him through the A-gap. All of our fullback paths appear identical to the defense through the mesh point. After clearing the mesh point with the quarterback we are able to assign the fullback to several different tasks.

The fullback must step with his play side foot first. Making the first step slightly wider to clear the body of the quarterback is also acceptable. The fullback then works downhill at the pre-snap A-gap after taking his first step.

On all run plays the ball carrier must always receive the handoff with their inside elbow up so they do not contact the quarterback.

The dive must hit fast. This is the key to success for any option dive. The quarterback is four yards behind the football and the fullback is one yard behind him. This alignment in Figure 48 promotes a fast hitting dive. Sometimes we put the fullback slightly more than one yard behind the quarterback while other times the fullback is slightly less than one yard behind. The slight variance is to account for the size of the steps of different backs. This allows the fullback to get to the mesh point quickly when the quarterback steps down hill upon receiving the snap.

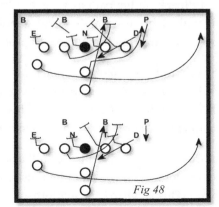

Most triple options come from under center because teams want the dive to hit the line of scrimmage quickly. A fast hitting dive forces the defense to make quick choices in regards to who will defend it. This hasty decision often leads to defensive mistakes and big yardage gains. It also leads to definitive defensive reactions that make the decisions of the quarterback easier. Shotgun option doesn't negate quick hit advantage.

Fig 48

The fullback in Figure 48 moves toward the line of scrimmage at the snap of the ball to maintain the quick speed of play. The fullback will clamp down on the ball if it is still in his belly once he has passed the front foot of the quarterback.

The fullback reads level one and works to level two upon the snap. The level one read is a block on the near defensive tackle. This determines where the fullback inserts into line of scrimmage. The level two read for the fullback is based on how the pulling guard blocks the play side linebacker.

Midline Dive

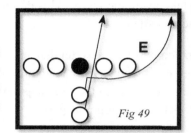

Power also provides the option to execute a tight fullback path in the form of a midline dive (Figure 49). We use this when defensive ends attempt to show the quarterback a give read before collapsing to the dive. Dives that hit tighter to the center makes the defensive end react faster. This forces the defensive end to make a decision sooner than desired.

Fig 49

Fullback Load

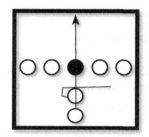

Power also features a "Load" fullback path. After the dive fake is completed the fullback veers outside to block the defensive end. The fullback in Figure 50 tries to log block the defensive end and will react to kick him out if needed.

Fig 50

POSITION FUNDAMENTALS

Quarterback Fundamentals

The quarterback's first step is to the outside leg of the center with his play side foot. The second step brings him square to the fullback and the A-gap dive path he is on. On his second step he also pushes the ball to his back hip, thus presenting it to the pocket (stomach and arms) of the fullback. The quarterback must meet the fullback on his path as he is headed to the line of scrimmage. He does not want to push the fullback wider than his own path. The quarterback also does not want to appear too shallow with his body positioning making him unable to properly seat the ball in the stomach of the dive back.

The quarterback's feet are angled into the line of scrimmage. This establishes an attacking demeanor that sets him up for a fast departure into the pitch phase. The quarterback will be slow to get the ball to the alley where the pitch phase develops if his feet are not set toward the line of scrimmage. Any slight delay in reaching the pitch phase is detrimental to big play potential.

The ride of the mesh with the fullback is carried to the front foot of the quarterback. Once the ball gets to the quarterback's front foot he must either leave the ball with the fullback or take it from him to the pitch phase. This is where the quarterback is forced to make a decision. If the quarterback keeps the ball for the pitch phase we describe the next task as attacking the alley. This "attacking the alley" refers to the quarterback keeping the ball unless he is being tackled. The alley is the area outside of the dive key and inside of the pitch key.

The quarterback must have a plan of attack so he can be decisive and his thought process during the dive phase (Figure 51) is that the fullback gets the ball unless the dive key is going to tackle him. When the ball

is pulled from the fullback it is now the quarterback's ball until the pitch player commits to tackle him. These concepts refer back to the two-on-one fast break nature of option football. In a basketball application of football the quarterback is looking to "pass" the ball to his fullback teammate in the dive phase so he gets the layup.

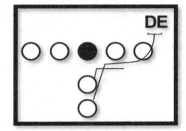

Fig 51

The critical coaching emphasis is on teaching the quarterback to get the ball to the fullback unless he is unable to do so. It is the quarterback's job to give the ball when a defender cuts off his path to the "basket." In this case he is "passing" the ball to his pitch back for the easy layup. It is extremely important that the quarterback understands the "fullback first" principle in triple option "fast break." The two-on-one advantage is lost without it.

When entering the pitch phase the plan of attack for the quarterback changes. This is now a two on one fast break and the quarterback will keep the ball for the layup unless he cannot get to the basket. If the pitch player cuts off his path he will pitch the ball to the pitch player. The quarterback will pitch the ball laterally or ever so slightly backwards. He will push his thumb down to create a soft tumbling effect on the football. Finally, he will trail towards the target. Trailing, or following, the pitch allows for accuracy and it removes the quarterback from harm's way.

Pitch Player Fundamentals

We do not motion our wing (or any other pitch player) to get them in the proper relationship because the Tex-Bone runs out of shotgun formations. The shotgun delays the execution of the play just long enough to allow the wing player to get into the right alignment relative to the quarterback. The pitch player must get going the instant that the ball is snapped for this to work however.

It is particularly important that the pitch player gains ground with his first step for this to alignment to occur properly. The pitch player aims for the feet of the quarterback. The quarterback steps down hill toward the line of scrimmage while getting out of the way of the pitch back. This step gives the pitch back a clear and tight path to get over the top of the play into the proper pitch relationship.

The pitch player in Figure 52 must receive the football going downhill. We do not want the pitch player to catch the ball running to the sideline. It is important to note that when the ball is pitched the pitch back needs to have already achieved adequate width for receiving the ball (four to five yards from the quarterback). The pitch back is then able to receive the ball running downhill towards the end zone when he achieves that adequate width. This is the ideal way to receive a pitch.

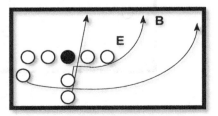

Fig 52

Playside Wing/Slot Fundamentals

The fundamentals of the play side wing/slot are very important. Against two high safeties the play side wing/slot releases immediately to the safety. Against a one high safety the play side slot or wing checks for a scraping linebacker out the box before releasing to the single safety.

The next two Figures (53 and 54) help illustrate these rules. The first illustration shows Shotgun Flexbone against a two high safety (Cover 4) defense. Offenses generally face a four-man defensive line/three linebacker look in Cover 4. Setting up in this formation makes it difficult for the middle linebacker to scrape far enough toward the play that the pulling guard is able to reach him. This allows the wing to work directly to the play side safety. The play side safety is an immediate threat to the play and needs accounting for. This puts the two high safety rule in place.

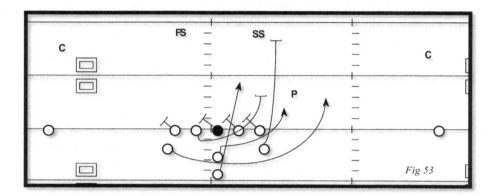

Fig 53

The two high safety rule is the same whether a wing or slot is set to the play side. Figure 54 shows the play side blocker as a slot receiver. The slot's role in this play is to go directly to the safety when there are two safeties high. This illustration shows the slot player gaining inside position before working inside out to the outside number of the safety. Notice how the illustration does not show the slot working toward the pitch player—it shows the slot establishing inside position (getting the ball behind him) before working to the safety. Getting to a position where the ball is behind him creates an advantage for the blocker.

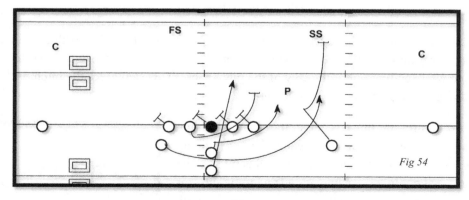

Fig 54

The next illustration (55) shows a one-safety (Cover 3) defense. A one safety and four down linemen defense means there are four linebackers. In this defensive alignment there is the potential for a play side linebacker scraping out of the box (past the reach of the pulling guard) and becoming a threat to the play. Against a single high safety defense the role of the play side wing/slot is to check for a scraping linebacker and then working to the single safety. This effectively combats the play side linebacker threat.

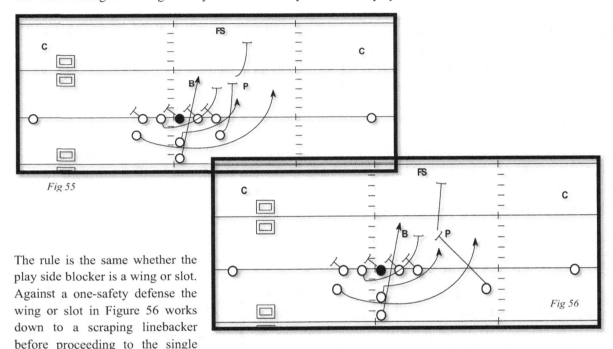

Fig 55

The rule is the same whether the play side blocker is a wing or slot. Against a one-safety defense the wing or slot in Figure 56 works down to a scraping linebacker before proceeding to the single safety. When checking for a scraping linebacker the wing/slot player must learn not to loiter. If the linebacker is not moving quickly toward him the pulling guard will be able to block him.

Offensive Line Fundamentals

The play side blockers execute down blocks in Power (Figure 57). This is true for the tackle, guard, and center. All of the play side linemen are looking first for any immediate gap threat. This is a 2 or 3-technique for the tackle. For the guard this is a 0, 1, or 2-technique

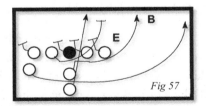

Fig 57

that attaches himself on the play. After seeking an immediate gap threat defender the play side linemen look for a looper. A "looper" is defined as a defensive lineman who slants to the gap they are responsible for.

The Tex-Bone treats all loopers the same as linebackers in order to remain gap sound. These defenders are identified and accounted for by down blocking anytime they encounter them on their path. If the pulling guard takes the job of picking up the looper when he comes through toward the play side linebacker it creates a situation where the front side linebacker is potentially unblocked. This is clearly not an ideal situation. For this reason gap-blocking linemen on the play side cannot over look loopers. Play side linemen work to the backside linebacker after checking the gap threat and looking for loopers to combat this concern.

It is critical that linemen gain ground with their first step. Our linemen work especially hard to train this skill. Failure to gain ground allows level one penetration, missed loopers, and missed level two linebackers.

Offensive lineman must anticipate linebacker movement. If an offensive tackle is facing a defense that deploys a 1-technique to his side of the line it is likely that he is able to work through to the backside linebacker. After taking a hard inside step (and checking for a looper) the offensive tackle then works to the backside linebacker. The tackle must anticipate that the backside linebacker will be moving toward him because when the pulling guard leaves the backside of the formation the gap departs with him and shifts to the play side.

Defenses often combat this adjustment by mirroring the guard's trade with a linebacker trade. If the tackle moving to level two doesn't anticipate this counter maneuver he runs the risk of heading to where the linebacker was instead of where he will be. The linebacker is potentially unblocked at the point of attack if the tackle doesn't aim for where the linebacker is going end up in this case.

The backside pulling guard executes a skip pull in Figure 57. A skip pull means the guard crosses his back foot behind his front foot in a skipping motion while moving laterally. We favor the skip pull because it allows the point guard to keep his shoulders and eyes facing forward. It also allows him to work more aggressively toward the end zone. We coach our players to always move towards the end zone with their shoulders square to the line of scrimmage. This allows the puller to reach his assignment faster.

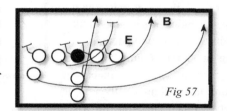

Fig 57

The pulling guard is looking for the first opening to insert into the play. Our goal (as previously mentioned) is to gain horizontal displacement across the line of scrimmage with our play side blockers. The offensive tackle is going to try to knock the 3 technique all the way past the center. This opens an easy path for the pulling guard to fit around the tackle and get to the play side linebacker.

The backside tackle is able to execute a base block or a hinge block. We game plan this block from week-to-week based on the method we think is more advantageous for our specific players or more advantageous against the defense we face. We want to know how the defense reacts to a hinge block or base block before making final plans or making in game adjustments. We also consider if our center will need help with his back block.

PLAYS BLOCKED FOR TOUCHDOWNS

An important differentiation to make between the Tex-Bone and other offenses is plays blocked for touchdowns and plays blocked for first downs. Triple option Tex-Bone plays are blocked for touchdowns. They use a numerical, fast break advantage to reach the end zone. One-back spread offense plays are blocked to achieve first downs.

Figure 58 shows a spread Power Read run play. Analyzing the difference in blocking philosophy is not an attempt to denigrate standard spread Power Read—the play is an element included in the Tex-Bone offense. The goal is to reveal some of the built-in limitations that standard spread Read must overcome to achieve large yardage gains. What you notice below is the one-back spread alignment allows both safeties to roam free and tackle the quarterback if the play goes up the middle off a pull read. The play side safety is equally free to make a tackle if the running back receives the ball on the sweep element of the Power Read.

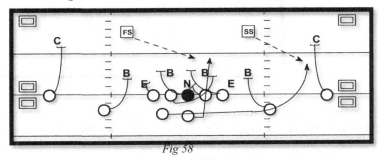

Fig 58

Plays like this are blocked for first downs rather than touchdowns. They gain yards and produce first downs in the open field. It is less likely that they yield a touchdown compared to a well-executed triple option play however. There are typically two (sometimes three) "free hitters" on the defense against a one-back spread formation whereas all play side defenders are accounted for in the Tex-Bone. Mistakes on defense create even larger gains in the triple option. Spread runs rely on defenders making mistakes or require an offensive player to beat an unblocked defender to a landmark on the field. The play ends when the defense adjusts or catches up. Tex-Bone plays continue to the end zone when properly executed.

Triple option plays account for all play side defenders by matching formations to the defense. Recognizing this difference between spread and the triple option is critical. The Tex-Bone pushes any "free hitters" as far away from the ball as possible and never at the point of attack. Accounting for everyone on defense is impossible because an offensive player always possesses the ball and is attacking the defense downfield. Triple option allows you to better control the location of the "free hitter".

The next two Figures (59 and 60) show a Flexbone option play against two different defensive structures. Similar to the last illustration this is also a Power run play. Pay particular attention to how all of the play side defenders are accounted for. Two players are being optioned in triple option football. What this means is the offense is not physically blocking two defensive players. The speed and attacking nature of the play force defensive choices that negate the need to block the two defenders individually. This allows us to pick up an additional block at the point of attack. The extra blocker gives option plays a better chance of reaching the end zone than its one-back spread cousin.

45

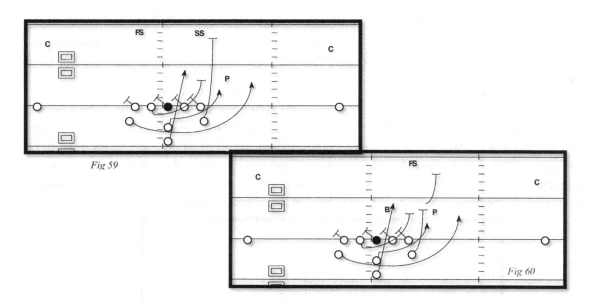

Fig 59

Fig 60

The same is true when running triple option from spread. Splitting a wing out to a slot position does not mean a safety is left unblocked. Because we option the play side linebacker the slot is free to work to the safety (see Figures 61 and 62). This increases the chance the play results in a touchdown. Naturally a defender is unblocked somewhere on the field. The triple option advantage is this unblocked defender is farther away from the ball than in most one-back formations.

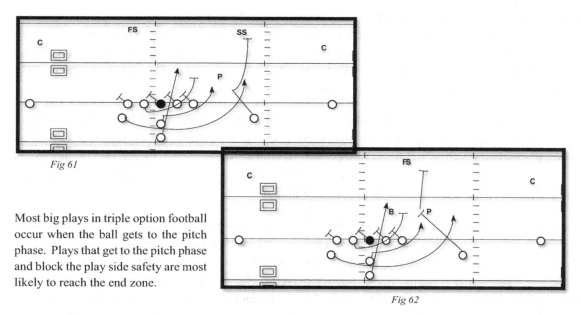

Fig 61

Most big plays in triple option football occur when the ball gets to the pitch phase. Plays that get to the pitch phase and block the play side safety are most likely to reach the end zone.

Fig 62

CH 6: G LOAD OPTION

G LOAD OPTION: the Swiss Army Knife of the Tex-Bone

G Load ("Belly" as it is known to some) began life as part of the original Delaware Wing T offense developed by coaches Dave Nelson and Tubby Raymond in the 1950s. It began as a lead before becoming a triple option play. As a lead-blocked play the "G Load" was a precursor to the earliest speed option sets. The diagram in Figure 63 shows the G Load block—a fold block between the play side guard and tackle taking place on the front side of the play. It is called a "load" play because the guard lead-blocks on the defensive end after pulling.

Early versions of Belly featured a dive fake that influence and accounted for the play side linebacker. In these plays the pitch phase worked to the play side linebacker specifically.

Tex-Bone G Load Option

G Load Option is the Swiss Army Knife of the Tex-Bone. I refer to this play as the Swiss Army Knife of the offensive because the dive player is always blocked. This effectively combats defenses that make the dive read difficult or play the dive in multiple ways. The G Load is tool to handle any technique a defense uses to defend the dive. The pressure to make the right ball distribution decision is removed from the quarterback because the play side guard is always blocking the dive key.

The play also slows backside linebacker pursuit because there is no backside guard pull. This is a contrast to Power Option where a puller is always added to the front side of the play.

Benefits of G Load Option

G Load Option is good against every front or blitz so there are no checks required, ever.

G Load Option is a rule based play. Slanting defensive linemen, multiple defensive fronts or structure,

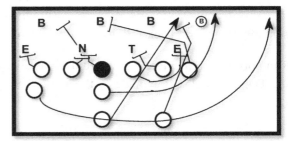

Fig 63

multiple blitzes, etc. do not throw players off once they internalize the rules of the scheme. This play produces success in all situations once your players understand the rules and techniques of G Load.

G Load Option offers natural play-action progressions. A quarterback carrying out the G Load Option fake creates an enticing situation for defensive players. Play action passes become available once defenders are sucked in by the option fake. Tex-Bone play action plays are discussed in greater detail later in the book.

G Load Option Assignments

The play side tackle's assignment in Figure 64 is B-gap to backside linebacker. If there is a 3-technique defensive lineman in the B-gap he takes it. The tackle works to the backside linebacker if there is no defensive tackle aligned in the B-gap and no player slants to the B-gap.

The play side guard pulls for the contain player. This is the load-block that gives the play its names. The goal is to always log the dive key, every play. If the puller is unable to log the defensive end he reacts and kicks the defensive end out. The fullback and quarterback follow this visual cue and react to the kick out.

The center blocks the play side A-gap to the backside linebacker. The backside guard is the opposite A-gap player. This center/guard combo manages the A-gaps and the backside linebacker.

The backside tackle is inside-out man-to-man on the defense end. A team is able to man block or hinge block this defensive end. The decision is based on offensive personnel strengths and the opponent. An important consideration in game planning is how a defense potentially reacts to both the base block and the hinge block.

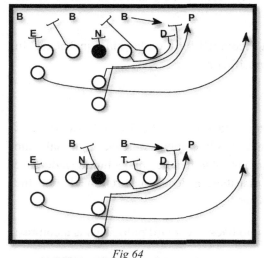

Fig 64

Just like any other triple option play the fullback dives to the A-gap. After the dive mesh the fullback picks up the filling or scraping play side linebacker on the outside.

The backside wing is a pitch back option for this play. A front side wing or front slide slot receiver is also able to serve as the pitch back option.

The quarterback rides the fullback through the dive mesh. Naturally there is no dive to read in terms of giving or keeping the ball. The quarterback looks at the dive key regardless. This is done because the dive key tells the QB whether he is taking the ball underneath the kick out block or around a log block by the play side guard. The fullback then takes the same path as a response to the guard's block. Essentially the quarterback follows the fullback as the play progresses toward the pitch player.

It is important to remember that the fullback is always a blocker on this play when the dive serves as token fake. There is no decision made by the quarterback in terms of whether the ball is given to the fullback or not.

G Load vs. Blitz

Nothing changes when a team faces defensive pressure in Figure 65. The G Load becomes easier to execute against an edge blitz because the log block is simplified for the pulling guard. All of the rules are the same across the offensive front. The play side tackle want to avoid getting caught up on the defensive tackle that is spiking to the B-gap. The goal is to get the tackle through his gap to the backside linebacker (who is likely coming towards the tackle in an attempt to cover the fullback). When the defensive dive key takes the inside gap away it creates an easy log

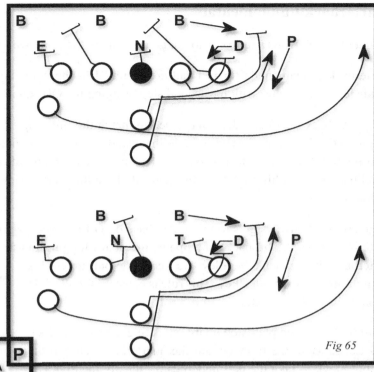

Fig 65

situation for the pulling play side guard.

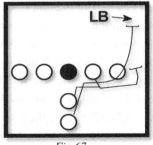

Fig 66

This also creates an easy opportunity for the fullback to release to the play side linebacker off the dive fake.

It's not necessarily a problem if the tackle gets caught up with the pinching dive key. The tackle stays on the dive key while the guard works to level two in search of any defender coming the from the backside. This on the fly adjustment essentially becomes an assignment trade between the guard and tackle.

POSITION FUNDAMENTALS

Fullback Fundamentals

All dives feature an A-gap aiming point for the fullback. The fullback in Figure 66 starts by stepping with his play side foot to make sure he doesn't run into the quarterback. The fullback follows this aiming point until he gets through the mesh point and is clear of the quarterback's front foot. The fullback then reacts to the play side guard once the fake is completed. He

Fig 67

works around the end if the guard is able to log the dive key. If the guard kicks out the fullback makes an adjustment to come underneath on his way to the play side linebacker.

Quarterback Fundamentals

The Quarterback reads and reacts to the guard's block the same way as the fullback in Figure 67.

Quarterback fundamentals for G Load are identical to those for Power Option. The first step is to the outside leg of the center with the second step bringing the QB square to the A-gap and the fullback's path.

The quarterback's feet and demeanor need to match the fullback's demeanor as he approaches the A-gap. The quarterback first meshes with the fullback and carries out the fake as if he is making a ball distribution determination (even though it is token). The quarterback then puts the ball on the fullback's stomach as the fullback reaches his back hip. In the third phase the quarterback then rides the fake all the way to his front foot.

The quarterback always gets to the pitch phase on G Load because the pull is prescribed. On G Load the quarterback (like the fullback) anticipates the guard logging the dive key and reacts to a kick out. The quarterback then attacks the alley and keeps the ball unless his path it impeded by the pitch key. This rule is constant for all triple option plays in the Tex-Bone.

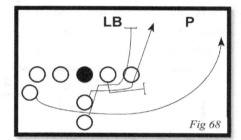

Fig 68

Figure 68 shows the play side guard executing a kick out block on G Load. Both the fullback and the quarterback react to the kick out block to take the ball underneath. Ideally the dive key is always logged. This is not always a possibility however.

The kick out doesn't mean the pitch phase is dead. A pitch to the back is possible even if the ball is taken underneath.

Pitch Fundamentals

Pitch fundamentals for G Load are the same as all option plays. When coming from the backside the pitch player gains ground with his first step. In the Tex-Bone it is important to remember that the pitch player is not motioned before the snap to get him in relationship. Some Tex-Bone plays actually motion the pitchman away from the pitch key before the ball is snapped. For this reason it is essential that the pitch player gain ground on this first step and aim for quarterback's feet. At the snap the quarterback steps down hill and out of way out of the pitch player coming around to get into proper pitch relationship. The pitch player needs to attain the adequate width needed as fast as possible in order to work

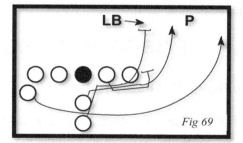

Fig 69

downhill and receive the pitch while working through the line of scrimmage and towards the end zone. The pitch player needs to be four (but no more than five) yards away from the quarterback when the ball is delivered to him (see Figure 69).

Playside Wing/Slot Fundamentals

It is important to remember that blocking rules stay the same regardless of whether the front side player is a wing or a slot. In the Tex-Bone the front side blocker immediately releases to the safety against two safeties high (as in Figure 70). We do this to keep the play side safety from running unchecked against the option.

The play side blocker (whether a wing or slot) is responsible for a linebacker scraping from inside the box before releasing to the safety in the middle of the field versus a one high safety defense.

The illustration below shows the Flexbone against a two high safety defense. The play side wing is shown releasing directly to the play side safety accordingly.

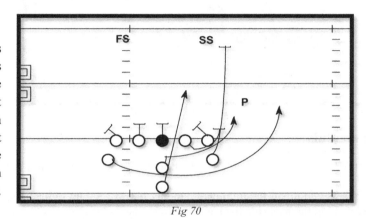

The release is executed the same way if the offense is in a spread formation. Notice how Figure 71 does not show the slot player working to block the pitch player first. It shows the slot player working to gain leverage on the safety while getting the ball behind him before working to the outside number.

Fig 70

There is a chance the play side linebacker scrapes over the top to reach the point of attack against a one-safety look. In Figure 72 the wing is able work to the single middle safety after checking the linebacker.

Fig 71

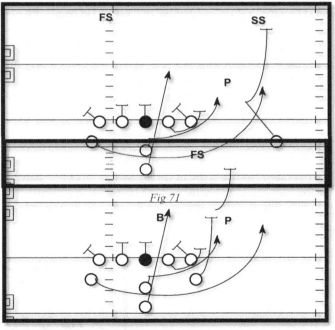

A similar situation occurs when running from the spread. The slot receiver in Figure 73 first looks for a scraping linebacker coming out of the box before working to the single middle safety if there is no linebacker to account for.

Fig 72

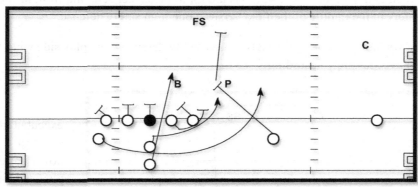

Fig 73

Offensive Line Fundamentals

The study of offensive line fundamentals begins with a look at the frontside fold block in Figure 74.

The tackle's primary emphasis is gap threat by alignment and any player looping to his gap. From there the emphasis transitions to blocking the backside linebacker. He is first and foremost a B-gap player.

The tackle's assignment is easy if he faces a 2 or 3-technique defender. He begins by down blocking the defensive tackle with the goal of attaining as much lateral movement down the line of scrimmage as possible. If the tackle has no immediate defensive tackle to block he looks for a looping 0 or 1-technique defender. The 0 or 1-technique is then blocked if encountered. If nothing materializes the tackle takes an angle towards level two—anticipating that the linebacker may scrape towards him. Note that the tackle is not waiting around to see what happens. If he has no threat by alignment and no threat by a looper he stays on track to level two.

The guard simultaneously works to log the dive key. We always want to log this player. If the dive key releases wide and outside we react to this on the fly to locate and kick out. The center is working with the backside guard and tackle. They combine to reach the near play side or backside defensive tackle while also accounting for the backside linebacker and defensive end. This creates an advantageous three-on-three scenario. The tackle is thinking man-to-man against the defensive end unless a blitz forces him to commit to protecting the B-gap on the inside.

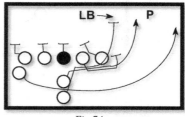

Fig 74

CH 7: DOUBLE PULL POWER

The smash-mouth play of the Tex-Bone

The Origin of Double Pull Power

Double Pull Power traces its roots to the Double Wing Power Toss. The Double Wing was first credited to Pop Warner in the 1910s. Many other offenses (the Wishbone, the Flexbone, etc.) were developed around this formation in the years to follow. The Double Pull Power (often called "Super Power" at the youth level) features a play side double team with two pullers from the backside. The guard and tackle pull from the backside when "Super Power" is ran out of the double wing (Figure 75).

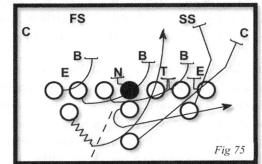

Fig 75

Tex-Bone Double Pull Power

To goal of Double Pull Power is to get a strong play side double team. For this reason we refer to it as the smash-mouth play of the Tex-Bone. The two pullers allow for a play side double team and vertical displacement. Most of the displacement in the Tex-Bone is horizontal along the line of scrimmage. This allows for an open area at the point of attack where pullers are able fit their blocks appropriately. In Double Pull Power we use a heavy double team to create a cratered line of scrimmage at the point of attack that the ball is run behind.

Benefits of Double Pull Power

The benefits of Double Pull Power are many. First, there are multiple ball carriers. Illustrations later in the chapter show some of the different ball carrier options.

There are multiple formations options for Double Power Pull.

Double Power Pull features built in play-action protection. (Play action combinations accompanying Double Power Pull are detailed in later chapters.)

Double Pull Power is good against every defensive front. There is no need to check the play to something else because blitzing linebacker protection is built in.

Double Pull Power is a rule based play (similar to many others in the Tex-Bone). Players effectively handle all defensive formations, line movements, and blitzes once they understand the rules of the play.

Quarterback Double Pull Power (with or without a Tight End)

Figure 76 shows Double Pull Power with a tight end. The play side tackle leads the combination block with the guard or the tight end against the nearest defensive lineman. The combo is with the guard against a 3-technique. Against a 5 or 7-technique defensive end the combo is with the tight end. In Double Power Pull the tackle is involved in a double team block whenever possible—regardless of the defensive alignment. There is always a double team with a tight end.

The play side guard block depends on the situation. Options include (1) solo blocking the A-gap or (2) combo blocking against a B-gap 2 or 3-technique defender (as detailed above). The center then back blocks the first player he encounters, the backside guard pulls for the play side linebacker, and the backside tackle works inside-out man-to-man on the defensive end. These center, backside guard, and backside tackle rules are fixed for all power run plays. The play is base blocked or a hinge blocked based on who your tackle is and who he is playing against. The critical factor to remember is that on the backside of the offensive line this play is identical to all other Tex-Bone Power plays. This familiarity breeds confidence and aggression.

The play side of the Double Pull Power features some adjustments from the base Power set. The adjustments are made with the intent of executing a double team on an inside player whenever possible. As the name implies this Power play features a second puller comes from the backside. The illustration shows the backside wing in the second puller role. (Depending on the formation another second puller option is the running back.) The backside wing pulls around for the backside linebacker while the play side wing takes either the play side outside linebacker or the defensive end (depending on the location of the double team).

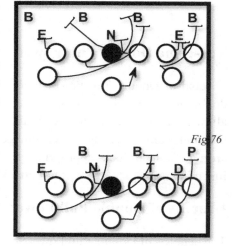

Fig 76

In tight end formations the tight end blocks the defensive end. This block is either a single man-on-man block or a double team based on what the tackle faces inside. The tight end blocks the defensive end man-on-man if the tackle is working inside to double team the defensive tackle.

Figure 76 of Quarterback Double Pull Power with a Tight End features two different scenarios for the double team block.

Scenario one: the tackle and tight end double-team if there's a 5 or 7-technique defense end. Scenario two: the tackle and guard double-team if there is a 3 technique or a 2-technique defensive tackle. The play side guard follows normal Power rules (covering A-gap to backside linebacker) when he is not executing a double team.

The backside is standard Power football. The center back-blocks the nearest defender while the backside guard pulls for the play side linebacker and the backside tackle blocks inside-out man-to-man on the defensive end. An offense chooses a base block or hinge block based on their offensive strengths and opponent weaknesses.

The second puller to the play side is the backside wing. This pull is done by a running back depending on the formation. The backside linebacker is not accounted for by offensive linemen because of the play side double team.

In tight end formations the play side wing is always assigned to the play side outside linebacker. These rules potentially change when there is no Tight End. In those cases the play side wing is usually assigned to the defensive end.

Figure 77 explores the play side rules of Double Pull Power with no Tight End. The play side wing works opposite of where the tackle blocks. The tackle still blocks a hypothetical double team even without the Tight End. (In tight end formations the tackle double-teams with him on the defensive end.)

The bottom of the illustration shows a tackle double team against the 3-technique with the guard. The wing then picks up the defensive end as the tackle works inside to execute the double team. To do so the wing must identify or get a call from a tackle indicating where the block is going. This contrasts with the wing taking the outside linebacker when the tackle blocks the defensive end in the top diagram.

Both illustrations show Fullback Double Pull Power. The quarterback reverses out to get the ball to the fullback quickly. He then faces the line of scrimmage and set up as if to pass.

The ball carrier takes a side step regardless of whether it's the fullback or the quarterback. This side step serves two purposes: (1) it gets the ball carrier behind the double team—this allows the ball carrier to work downhill, cutting off the defensive movement created by the double team and (2) it creates time for the pullers backside guard and wing to locate the inside

Fig 77

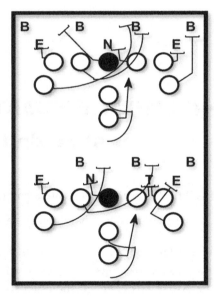

coming from the linebackers.

Double Pull Power vs. Blitz

Defensive pressure is not a huge concern in Pull because all linebackers are accounted for. A option is always a good option if desired. Figure option checks from typical Double Pull Power

The fullback becomes the pitchman depending A team is able to bring the wing around to pitchman if there is no fullback in the game. speed option is always a good choice regardless By no means does a team need to check into when facing pressure however.

Double Power check to speed 78 shows speed looks.

on the formation. become the Changing to a of the formation. speed option

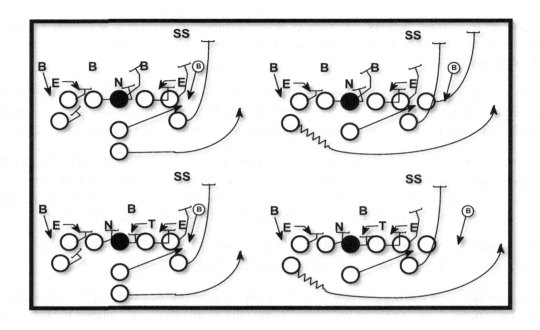

Fig 78

THE EMPTY FORMATION THAT CAN'T BE
(or shouldn't be) BLITZED

"Empty" Double Pull Power formations are a natural dissuasion for the blitz. The Tight End double wing empty formation in particular is one that defenses wants to avoid blitzing. Here's why...

There are six players left to account for gaps in the run defense *after* they account for the five eligible receives (two split ends, two wings, one tight end). This leaves an open gap. Figure 79 shows a double edge blitz with the A-gap left open. If the defensive tackle pinches to play the A-gap it leaves the B-gap open. This shift creates an open gap in the run fit that the offense is able to take advantage of.

Fig 79

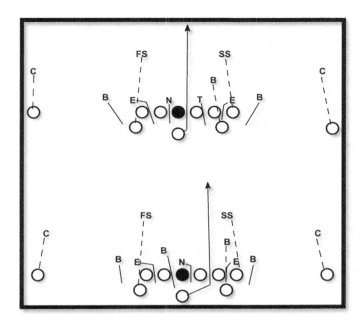

Defensive coaches might counter this problem by assigning a linebacker to both gap protection in the run game and vertical pass coverage. This dual role for the LB is extremely challenging—and exploitable. The linebacker is then left with a difficult choice. Running with an offensive player releasing vertically downfield opens a gap for the run game. Blitzing or committing to his run gap responsibility gives the offensive player a free release downfield. Committing to the blitz creates an even greater problem by weakening run gap protection *and* giving free release to eligible receivers. Blitzing this formation is extremely risky for the defense. That is precisely why we utilize it frequently.

POSITION FUNDAMENTALS

Ball Carrier Fundamentals

The first step for the ball carrier is a slide towards the A-gap. The slide step achieves the goals of timing the ball carrier's entry at the point of attack while keeping him square to the line of scrimmage. The ball carrier is able to effectively read the double team once he is in the right place, at the right time, and facing the proper direction.

Fig 80

The double team against the 3-technique is detailed in Figure 80. The bottom of the illustration shows the double team against the defensive end. The ball carrier stays inside the double team for both blocks unless the block washes down into the path of the ball carrier.

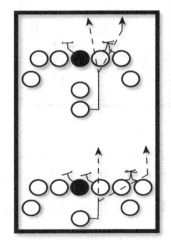

Remember, the point of the double team in smash-mouth Double Pull Power is getting vertical displacement. This contrasts with other Tex-Bone plays that are designed to wash defenders horizontally down the line of scrimmage. The proper path for the ball carrier is inside the vertical push of the double team so he is running towards the end zone instead of turning his shoulders and running to the sideline.

In other cases the ball carrier bounces the play outside the double team when the 3-technique is washed down the line of scrimmage. These cuts do not go "against the grain" (a drastic change in direction) as much as they initially appear however. The lateral distance of this cut is a much shorter in person than they look on paper. This cut by the ball carrier happens when the double team washes down to the inside.

Play Side Wing Fundamentals with No Tight End

Previous sections explained that the tight end always blocks the defensive end. But what happens when there is no tight end? Without a tight end the play side wing identifies where the tackle blocks. The wing then takes the defensive end if the tackle blocks inside (top of Figure 81). The scenario flips when the tackle blocks outside (bottom of Figure 81).

Blocking properly without a Tight End appears difficult on the surface. A simple call by the tackle makes sure the wing blocks the correct defender. Wings learn their blocking assignments relatively quickly through repetitions in practice.

The first step of the play side wing is always inside. This establishes a position allowing the blocker to work inside-out to the outside number of the intended target. The goal is to run the ball inside. If the wing were to work outside first he would run the risk of allowing a defender to get inside of him. This is why we want the wing to work inside first. It is not likely that the outside backer becomes a threat to the play if he fills off the edge—especially if the wing adjusts his path to get to the linebacker late.

Playside Wing Fundamentals with a Tight End

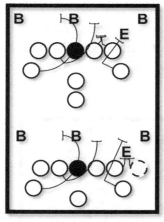

Fig 81

The play side wing works to the play side outside linebacker whenever a Tight End is aligned to the play side of the formation. The wing knows he is able to bypass the defensive end because it's always the tight end's job to block him.

The wings in Figure 82 steps down inside first. This allows him to establish a position with the ball behind him as he works inside out to the linebacker.

Backside Wing Fundamentals

The backside wing then pulls for the backside linebacker. It is important that the backside wing gains ground with the first step and stays square to the line of scrimmage. Some of our wings even pick up the skip pull technique that our guards execute.

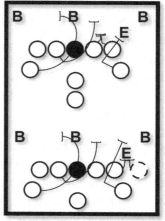

Fig 82

The top of Figure 82 shows the backside wing's movement without a Tight End. The bottom of Figure 82 shows his movement with a Tight End.

Double Team Fundamentals

The double team always occurs on the first player outside the guard. This rule makes it simple for the tackle to understand his assignment. Both players step together on the double team. We coach our players to get their hips together and make a vertical push. This again is a departure from other

58

Tex-Bone plays where the intent is to get movement horizontally down the line of scrimmage. On this play we're looking for vertical displacement.

The top portion of Figure 82 shows the double team without a tight end. The bottom portion shows the double team with a tight end.

The outside player comes off the double team when facing a slanting or pinching defender. The guard stays with a 3-technique that is attempting to slant to the A-gap and takes him down inside. The tackle then blocks base Power and works up to the second level backside linebacker.

WILDCAT DOUBLE PULL POWER

Figures 83 and 84 show some fun variations to the Double Power Pull scheme.

Double Pull Power works well as a wildcat formation. Starting the quarterback in the backfield before fast motioning him to the slot right before the snap is one way to execute Wildcat Double Power Pull. This motion draws attention from everyone outside the box by pulling the outside linebacker and safety out wider. The defensive shift gives the fullback a nice seam to run through once he reaches the second level.

Another option is to lineup in empty. The quarterback in this set lines up in the slot where he draws defensive attention as a double pass threat. Bubbling the quarterback to the boundary creates an advantage by displacing a linebacker and drawing the attention of the safety. Bubbling also keeps the quarterback out of harm's way during the play.

Empty Double Wing Power Pull is not a set bound to the wildcat exclusively. Teams are able to run it with a quarterback if desired. Run it out of wildcat if that creates an advantage or use your quarterback if that creates an advantage. Both looks work effectively when used with your best personnel.

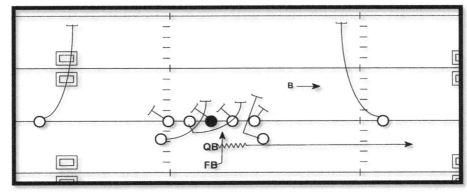

Fig 83

MOTION DOUBLE PULL POWER

The Tex-Bone also likes Double Pull Power with Jet motion (Figure 84). The addition of Jet motion creates two specific advantages: (1) Linebackers are forced to move laterally when the ball is snapped instead of working downhill and (2) Jet motion induces rolling coverages and other pre-snap defensive movements that distract secondary defenders. Defenders moving laterally or rotating at the snap creates an instant advantage when running a smash-mouth Power play. This split second confusion or change in movement gives the offense a head start downfield.

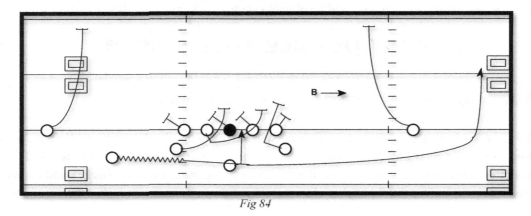

Fig 84

CH 8: SPEED OPTION

SPEED OPTION: the solution to pressure and line games in the Tex-Bone

The Origin of Speed Option

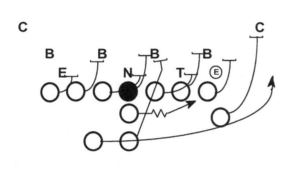

The Speed Option originated with coaches that ran Outside Veer and Belly schemes. An early iteration shown at the top of Figure 87 used a token fake to the fullback. Scraping linebackers eventually created the need to lead the fullback around the edge however (bottom of Figure 87).

The University of Nebraska famously ran Speed Option from the "I" formation in the 1980s and 1990s. The top of Figure 88 shows Speed Option in the "I" formation. One-back spread offenses ultimately eliminated the lead block altogether. The bottom of figure 88 shows Speed Option from a spread formation.

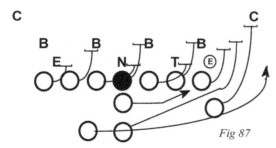

Fig 87

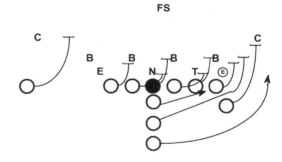

Fig 88

Benefits of Speed Option

Speed Option is a form of Outside Zone in the Tex-Bone offense. For us this means using reach and overtake (scoop) blocking techniques. The contain player of the defense becomes the unblocked pitch key in Tex-Bone Speed Option.

Speed Option heavily dissuades pressure and line games. The play gets to the edge of the defense quickly when a reach and overtake outside zone scheme options the contain player. The defense then finds itself outnumbered if defenders are twisting or looping away from the point of attack. Overtake blocking schemes

62

help alleviate the pressure created by defensive pressure or line games. Anyone that loops away from the play is not a concern because they are moving away from the ball.

Speed Option is available from different formations and with any personnel grouping. This chapter details multiple ways the Speed Option concept is executed.

Speed Option also provides an additional advantage of creating multiple backfield alignment options as well.

SPEED OPTION WITH A WING

Figure 89 shows the play side tackle bypassing the contain player and releasing to the second level in Speed Option when a wing is in the game. The angle he takes depends on defensive end alignment. The tackle releases outside to the second level if the defensive end is tight or inside if the defense end is aligned wide. Film study and coaching provides the training tackles needs to consistently make the right choice in terms of an inside or outside release.

The play side guard's responsibility is to reach the play side B-gap. The guard overtakes and works to level two if he faces a gap threat. The center then works with the guard to reach and overtake (full scoop) a 3-technique. (Reaching a full gap over is generally not a problem for our linemen.)

We execute the same full scoops across the entire line of scrimmage on Speed Option. The fullback aligned behind the quarterback is the pitch player and the play side wing works to the play side outside linebacker. The quarterback then attacks the outside number of the contain player and pitches the ball to the fullback at the earliest opportunity. Tight End responsibilities in Speed Option are the same as a split end. Similar to a split receiver this means blocking the deep coverage over the top. Play side Tight Ends are not a part of the scoop blocking scheme.

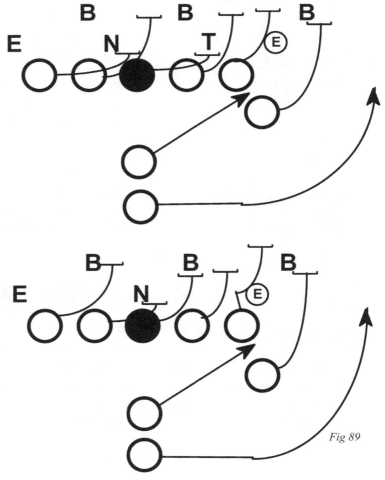

Fig 89

Spread Speed Option

Spread formations and personnel groups minimally affect the blocking scheme for Speed Option. Spread Speed Option is still a reach and overtake scheme with full scoops across the line of scrimmage. Figure 90 shows the tackle bypassing the contain player (the pitch key) and releasing to the second level. He then chooses an inside or outside release based on alignment of the defensive end.

A slot receiver replaces the wing in a Spread Speed Option look. His responsibilities remain the same however—block the play side outside linebacker.

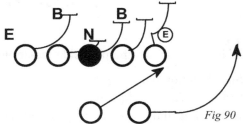

Fig 90

Speed Option vs. Blitz

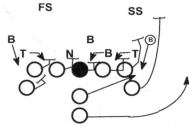

Fig 91

There are several choices in terms of blitz pickup when running Speed Option. Figure 91 shows situations where we keep the contain player as the pitch key. The contain player and pitch player are now the outside linebacker because of the double edge blitz.

The defensive end (who usually is the pitch player in most base defenses) now works inside to the B-gap and is the responsibility of the play side guard that is reaching the gap that the defensive end is slanting to.

The play side tackle still works to the second level and bypasses the defensive end and the blitzing contain player. Everyone else works to reach and overtake (full scoop). The quarterback's point of attack is now wider because the outside linebacker is the new pitch key.

POSITION FUNDAMENTALS

Pitch Back Fundamentals

The pitch relationship is extremely critical. The pitch back must gain ground with his first step to reach the right position whether he is aligned behind or next to the quarterback (we will utilize both). The pitch back's goal is to defeat the leverage of the defensive end as fast as possible. The quarterback should pitch the ball once this leverage is overcome (Figure 92).

We coach the pitch back to work to a distance of 4 to 5 yards from the quarterback. Most important to us is that the pitch back receives the ball moving downhill exactly as the illustration on the right demonstrates.

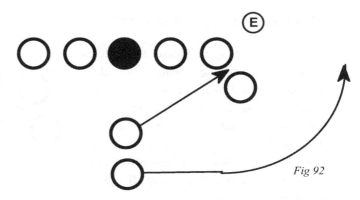

Fig 92

We want our pitch players to receive all pitches—no matter if it is a triple option or Speed Option—as flat as possible. Some option coaches talk about pitching the ball backwards. We do not want this negative relationship because the goal is avoid giving up yardage already gained during the pitch phase. This is why we want a flat pitch.

We sometimes pitch the ball slightly forward when we're behind the line of scrimmage. Pitches across the line of scrimmage are always sideways. Our quarterbacks are coached accordingly. It is important to remember that in the rules of football there is no such thing as a lateral (passes are either forward or backward). When coaching the backwards pitch we highlight the idea of the pitch being flat or sideways.

Quarterback Fundamentals

The number one concept for quarterbacks is that Speed Option is really Speed Pitch as far as they are concerned. The goal is to see how fast the quarterback is able to get the defensive end to commit and then make the pitch. The quarterback must gain ground on the first step and move directly towards the contain player's outside number in order to execute Speed Pitch properly.

The pitch back receives the ball as soon as the defensive end commits to containing the quarterback. This emphasis needs coaching over and over again so it becomes internalized and automatic for the quarterback. As soon as the pitch back defeats the leverage of the defensive end he should receive the pitch.

It is important for the quarterback to attack the outside number of the pitch key to prevent slow play (playing halfway between the running back and quarterback) from interfering with the developing exchange. We want to force the pitch key to make a definitive decision on whether he is taking the pitchman or the quarterback as early as possible.

A situation where the quarterback keeps the ball when the pitch key is a zone defensive end occurs extremely rarely. A defensive end occasionally takes a wide and fast uphill contain path that forces the quarterback to keep the ball. This occurs when the defense blitzes inside (using a double A-gap blitz for example).

On all option plays the quarterback must begin the play with a plan. It is important to emphasize that a quarterback keeper on Speed Option against a base defensive end pitch key is exceptionally rare. This is particularly true for teams that run triple option alongside to Speed Option. Teams that run triple option likely see a lot of defensive end contain players that close very quickly on inside releases by tackles. This results in easy ball distribution by the quarterback. The quarterback must first think, "I'm going to pitch this ball" and then react to a situation accordingly when a pitch isn't possible.

Play Side Wing Fundamentals

The play side wing in Figure 93 executes an arc release to the outside linebacker. This angle is inside-out to the outside number of the defender. The wing gains leverage to the outside and attacks towards the goal line when executing an arc release properly. A cut block is highly effective in the situation. In college football the cut block must take place within five yards of the line of scrimmage and must come from a vertical angle toward the defender.

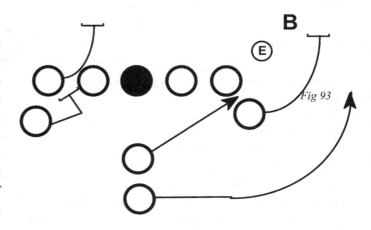

Satisfying the criterion for a legal cut block is fairly easy when an offensive player takes the right initial departure from the line of scrimmage.

When wings are aligned as a slot they maintain the same responsibility of blocking the play side outside linebacker. The difference is the slot player moves outside-in rather than inside-out to block the linebacker. Coaching note: cut blocks from an outside-in angle are illegal at all levels of football. The slot maintains an outside number aiming point on the defender when a cut block is not possible.

Backside Wing Fundamentals

Backside wings follow the same blocking rules as a backside tight end (Figure 93). His job is to reach block the gap vacated by the tackle that is leaving to cut-off level one pursuit players. The backside wing is not part of the scoop scheme as a pseudo-Tight End however. He is actually a C-gap player in Speed Option.

Offensive Line Scoop Block Fundamentals

Gaining ground with the first step is essential when reach blocking. We accept that this first step is often backwards slightly (even though we don't coach this technique explicitly). This is not a "bucket step" however. "Bucket steps" are backward steps that do not gain much width for our linemen. Our emphasis is not on getting depth behind the line of scrimmage. We set our pre-snap alignment as far back from the center as possible in order to already have depth. We coach our players to take an angle that allows a reach block even if a slightly backward step is needed.

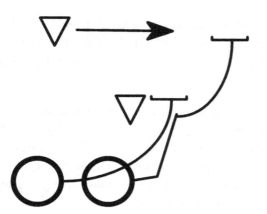

Fig 94

The "post" player in Speed Option is the covered player. He executes a technique in Figure 94 called "lane-ing" through" the defender on his way to the second level. The post player holds up the defensive linemen ever so slightly on his way to the linebacker. In the illustration the offensive linemen to the right is a post player. He takes a hard outside step and then works at a 45-degree angle through the outside shoulder of the defender. The post player working through to the second level gives his partner a chance to cross the face of a defensive lineman and complete the reach block.

The "lead" player in Speed Option follows a post player to complete the scoop block. He is responsible for completing the scoop of the level one defensive lineman. Angles are very important for both the post and lead player. We teach the critical importance of working at a 45-degree angle after taking their first steps at the line of scrimmage. Working at a 45-degree angle allows the post player to get to the linebacker and allows the lead player to gain leverage on the level one defender in order to reach and overtake.

Empty Speed Option

We like to run Speed Option from empty formations (see Figure 95). We especially like our Double Wing Empty formations in particular because they create a lot of variety in what we execute.

A major factor in us favoring empty formations is that our Double Wing Empty provides five immediate pass threats. This five-headed threat is particularly difficult for defenses to cover. We also like that we are able to run triple option, Speed Option, or anything else in the Tex-Bone arsenal in any direction from empty formations. We also like Double Pull Power from an empty formation.

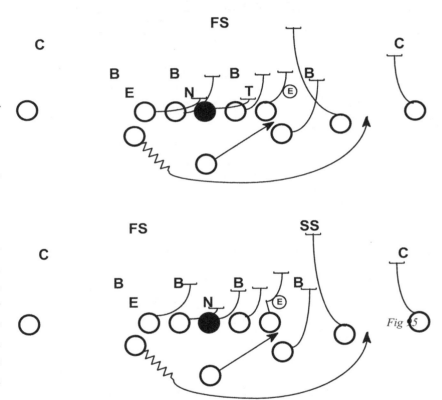

Fig 95

Speed Option to the perimeter is a great adjustment when teams load up the middle of the field. To execute Speed Option from a Double Wing Empty formation the wing that becomes the pitch back gets a slight head start before the ball is snapped. The short motion gives the wing all the time he needs to get around the quarterback and into pitch relationship.

Jet Motion Speed Option

Figure 96 shows Jet motion sweep with Speed Option blocking. The offensive linemen execute reach and overtake blocks similar other Speed Option looks. The play illustrated on the next page shows that instead of optioning the contain player, the running back out of the backfield executes a cut block on the level one defender. The Jet motion provides an added advantage by allowing quick access to the edge of the defense.

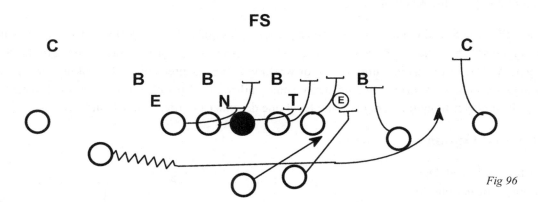

Fig 96

CHAPTER 9: POWER READ

POWER READ: diversity in the spread run game

Power Read Evolution

Power Read is the essential Power play of one-back spread football where the contain players is optioned instead of being blocked. (Traditional power formations block the contain player.) In Power Read the running back follows a sweep path across to face the quarterback with the quarterback serving as the dive back.

Tex-Bone Power Read

Power Read adapts the Tex-Bone's base option to spread formations and motions. Power Read is also available from option heavy formations as well. The Tex-Bone Power read is a double option play. This means the dive read become a give/keep sweep read and the pitch key is blocked. We only option the dive read on this play—not the pitch key. Optioning only the dive key is what makes this play a double option rather than a triple option.

Figure 97 shows Power Read in the Tex-Bone. This play features the same fundamental execution for the offensive line as a triple option Power play. The play side tackle is B-gap to backside linebacker and the play side guard is A-gap to back side linebacker. The center back-blocks the first defender encountered, the backside guard pulls to the play side linebacker, and the backside tackle is inside-out man-to-man on the defensive end. (This is the base-blocking scheme for all our Power looks.)

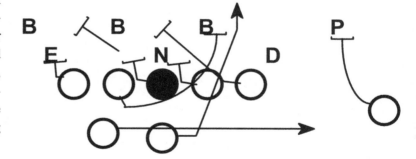

Power Read and Power triple option are not looking for any level one double-teams. The intent is to find horizontal displacement across the line of scrimmage rather than vertical displacement from a double team. This strategy is chosen because we want to make it easy for the dive player (in this case the quarterback) to insert into the line of scrimmage. We also want to

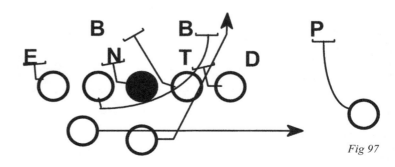

Fig 97

70

make it easy for the pulling guard to insert into the line of scrimmage. We do not want to force a dive player to go wide. Washing everything down the line goes a long way toward accomplishing these goals.

Washing the play horizontally allows for the dive to hit tighter to the A-gap. Doing this keeps the dive key from playing both the sweep and the dive. A double team block runs the risk of forcing the dive player wider—making a slow play by the defensive end even more problematic.

The running backs in Figure 97 are the sweep player crossing in front of the quarterback in Power Read. The quarterback reads the dive key to either give the ball to the sweep or pull and keep for an inside dive.

Power Read vs. Blitz

Power Read is a good play to combat defensive pressure. Changing the assignment of the play side tackle is the only adjustment needed against the blitz. The dive player is no longer being read in an edge blitz once the change is made. The play side tackle is assigned to man-to-man block the dive key instead. This adjustment makes the pitch key off the edge the new option key.

Quick note on making this play easy for your quarterback: teach them to identify the dive key and pitch key before every play. Reading dive and pitch keys are a skill that option quarterbacks need to develop. Running the option becomes far easier once dive and pitch keys are recognized before the snap. Identifying these defensive players helps the quarterback know when something doesn't look right and a change is needed. Power Read versus the blitz is an example of when an adjustment is needed.

Our players know that in blitzing situations the tackle takes the end (dive key) and the read is based off of the pitch key (linebacker). They know this because the quarterback makes a call at the line of scrimmage notifying the offensive tackle to adjust his block. Everyone else is executing Power football the same way they always do in the Tex-Bone.

The backside tackle in the two illustrations on the previous page takes the inside threat against a double edge blitz by blocking inside-out first. This means he takes any inside threat before working to any outside threat. Protecting the B-gap is as always a priority over the C-gap. The wide,

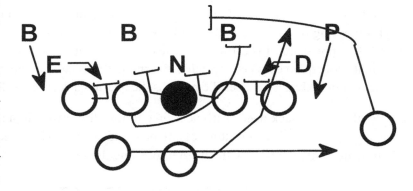

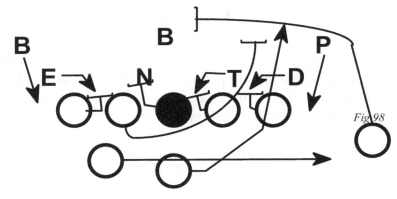

Fig 98

containment backside edge blitzer is left unblocked in a double edge blitz. The running back runs the sweep and the quarterback still runs the dive. The difference is the quarterback now looks at the pitch key for the give or pull indication.

The offense is able to look for two-on-one blocking situations against the blitz with a wing or slot in the game to the play side. Figure 98 shows two-on-one situations created by a Cover 0 (straight man to man). Even though there are no secondary players shown in the illustration we know this is a Cover 0 because there are seven defenders in the box. The un-pictured safety covering the slot player is always in man coverage. Releasing vertically and then moving inside to block the defender covering the running back man to man creates a situation where the slot blocks two players simultaneously (one physically, the other negated by chasing him away from the point of attack).

Picking up scraping linebackers against man coverage is extremely effective when attempting to get the ball to the perimeter of the defense. We also look for two-for-one's off of our inside crack blocks. These blocks are executed above the waist. (Cut blocks are illegal when working inside toward a defender.) Combined these adjustments give the Power Read an advantage against the blitz.

POSITION FUNDAMENTALS

Running Back Fundamentals

The running back must achieve full speed at the snap to mesh with and through the quarterback (Figure 99). This meshing occurs on the running back's third step. Aiming for the third step lets the back know where to align pre-snap. It is difficult for the defensive end to cross the line of scrimmage fast enough to take away the sweep (even when the defensive end is specifically assigned containment) when the running back takes off quickly and reaches the mesh as the quarterback receives the ball.

Naturally, the quarterback needs sufficient time to take the snap and present the ball to the running back. Any delay beyond this is a forfeiture of offensive advantage. The three-step mesh by the running back should provide optimal timing without compromising the speed needed to achieve large ground gains.

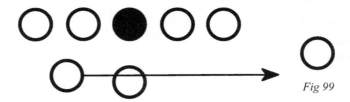

Fig 99

The sweep player must stretch the ball to the perimeter and run the same path whether receiving the ball or not. It is important for the sweep player to stretch the ball to the edge. The ball carrier cannot receive the handoff and quickly bend to the inside of the defense. Doing so contains the play on behalf of the defense and eliminates the offensive advantage.

Quarterback Fundamentals

Quarterbacks do not ride the mesh (move laterally) until the running back reaches them. This makes arriving together at the right time is critical. The dive key is able to play both the sweep and the dive if the quarterback slides too early. Quarterbacks must decide by their second shuffle whether to give the ball to the back or keep it. Additional shuffles get them too wide.

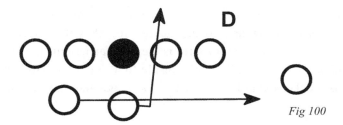

Fig 100

The quarterback in Figure 100 takes an inside dive path if he receives a pull read. Taking a tight, inside path the quarterback then reads the pulling guard for where to fit into level two. His job against the blitz is to alert the offensive line of blocking adjustments and change the read key. The offensive tackle now blocks the dive key (defensive end). The quarterback's primary read then becomes the pitch key for give or keep.

Quarterbacks must recognize the contain player as quickly as possible. They cannot make a quality read if this player is not identified immediately. A loss of yardage is likely if the quarterback fails to diagnose the blitz and adapt the read key accordingly.

Contain defenders spiking inside tell the quarterback to give the ball to the sweep player. The unblocked blitzing linebacker is free off the edge to tackle the sweep player for a loss however. Defenses attempt to cover both the sweep and the dive by running an edge blitz. Assigning the offensive tackle to block the dive key negates this scheme. This blocking adjustment leaves the quarterback with one player to read. The edge player is unable to cover both the sweep and the dive as a result.

Quarterbacks need an adjustment plan of action for all double option plays. Sending quarterbacks on the field without a plan is a mistake. Quarterbacks are slow with their execution if a plan for ball distribution isn't in place beforehand. This is because there are too many variables to analyze in real time and at game speed. (The same preplanning is needed for option pass plays as well.)

The quarterback's distribution plan on double option Power Read is to give the ball on the sweep unless the dive key is going to make the play. Pulling the ball to run the dive is done only when the sweep cannot reach the edge.

PERIMETER BLOCKING OPTIONS

There are several options for perimeter blocking. (All are discussed in greater length later.) Figure 101 shows formations with a three-player (three-for-three) blocking surface. Both include one split end. Figure 101 includes one slot receiver and one wing on top and two slot receivers on the bottom.

The base method for perimeter blocking is three-for-three on the nearest defender. Working inside-out to the defenders' outside number is particularly advantageous. It's okay if a linebacker wants to fill outside when facing an arc release. The worst-case scenario is the ball carrier cuts underneath the kick out block to gain yardage. The middle blocker usually works inside first to get the ball behind him. The safety is able to shoot inside of this blocker towards the line of scrimmage and make the tackle if the player starts too far outside.

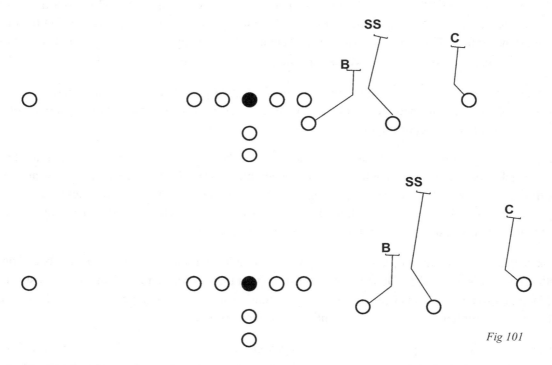

Fig 101

There are more options than blocking three-for-three on the nearest defenders of course. Figure 102 shows two inside players executing a cross block. The middle player then works inside for a crack block while the innermost player using an arc release to reach the safety. This scheme creates a nice ally for the ball carrier to follow.

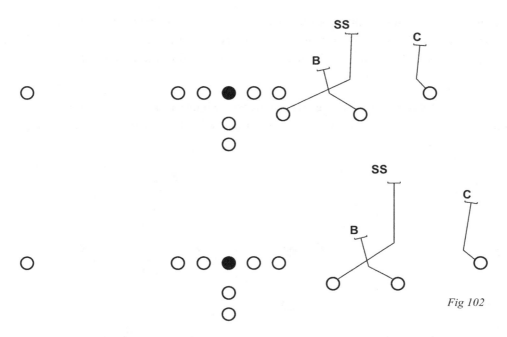

Fig 102

Figure 103 shows a cross blocking combo with two crack blocks and the inside player working out to the corner. The blocking path of the innermost player may look odd to some coaches initially. Both illustrations show the proper technique for taking an arc release that checks the outside linebacker before moving to the second level. After checking the outside linebacker he looks to see if the safety is secured before moving on to block the corner. It is an inside-out progression so the most dangerous defenders are secured in order of importance.

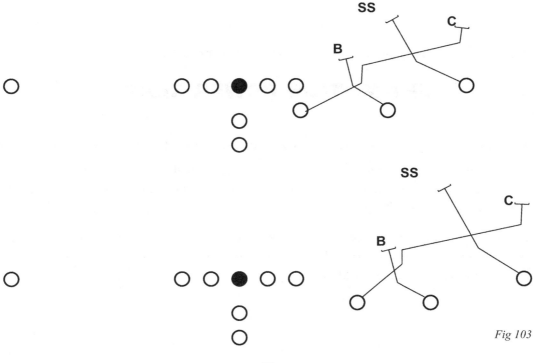

Fig 103

The progression of checking inside-out sets proper timing for when the inside receiver reaches and blocks the corner. Remember, the ideal time to engage any block is when the ball gets to the point of attack. We specifically want to match the timing of the inside receiver reaching the corner with when the ball gets there.

We are also able to cross block the outside two receivers. Figure 104 shows the innermost receiver arc blocking to the outside linebacker first. Cross blocking the second and third receiver then creates a seam between the corner and safety.

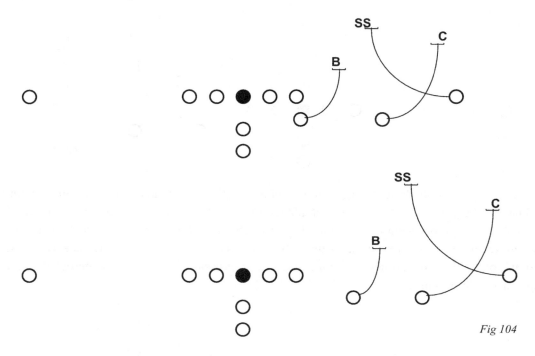

Fig 104

Additional information on perimeter blocking is provided in later chapters.

JET MOTION POWER READ

Jet Motion is one of the most effective ways to execute Power Read. The Jet motion player accelerates to full speed before the snap. The ball is snapped as he approaches the backside offensive tackle. The quarterback then gets just enough time to present the ball to the running back and make a decision on handing off or running the ball himself.

Our goal is to make it as difficult as possible for the dive key to cover the sweep. The speed at which Jet Motion Power Read hits at makes it extremely difficult for the dive player to stop the sweep from reaching the perimeter. Figure 105 illustrates Jet Motion.

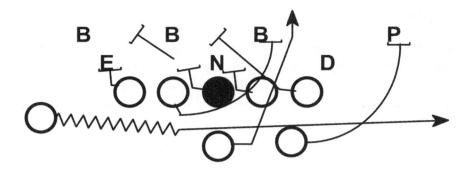

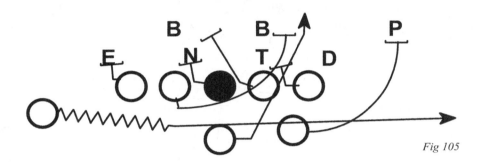

Fig 105

FLEXBONE POWER READ

Power Read is also available out of Flexbone. The Flexbone is a triple option heavy formation. Running speed sweep from this set is an excellent complement to Flexbone triple option.

The backside wing in Flexbone Power Read gets a head start before the snap on short motion—instead of coming in full speed motion. This head start (see Figure 106) allows him to arrive at the proper time to mesh with the quarterback. Wings gain an advantage by being able to move laterally before the snap without drawing a flag.

The running back in the backfield is the lead blocker on the pitch player in both Jet Motion and Flexbone Power Read. The fullback sets behind the quarterback in the Flexbone. Spread Power Read is slightly different with the running back lining up offset with the quarterback most frequently.

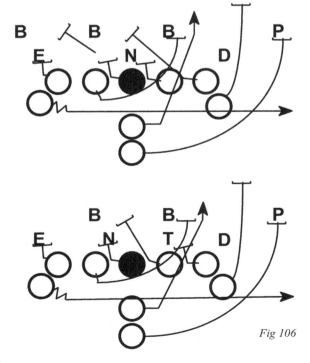

Fig 106

77

Wing blocking assignments

Wing blocking rules still apply. The wing works directly to the play side safety versus a two-high safety look. Versus a one high safety the wing checks for a scraping linebacker before moving to the single safety in the middle of the field. These rules are the same throughout the Tex-Bone system. They apply to the play side blocker whether he is a wing or a slot. The two diagrams in Figure 107 show these play side wing responsibilities.

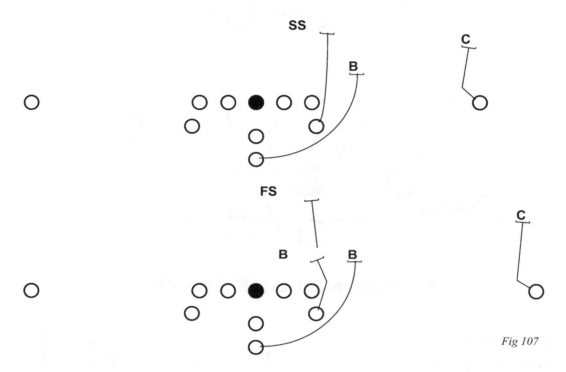

Fig 107

CHAPTER 10: VEER OPTION

VEER OPTION: traditional triple option
adapted to the Tex-Bone

Veer Option History

Split Back Veer ran from under center originated in the 1960s. The set is often credited to head coach Bill Yeoman at the University of Houston (Figure 108). Tom Osborne and the University of Nebraska also used Veer extensively from 1980s through the 1990s.

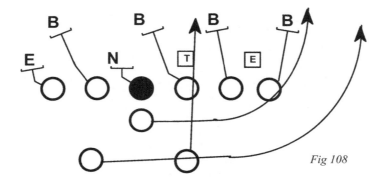

Fig 108

Outside Veer triple option gained notoriety in the 2000s at the University of West Virginia under head coach Rich Rodriguez (see Figure 109).

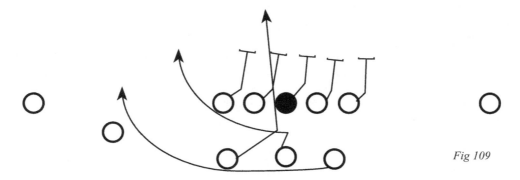

Fig 109

Tex-Bone Veer Option

Tex-Bone Veer Option is a standard option scheme adapted for shotgun and multiple formations. The Tex-Bone version runs a simple gap-control blocking scheme that looks similar to traditional veer option looks.

The Tex-Bone Veer Option works most effectively when ran toward an A-gap defensive tackle (2, 1, or 0-technique). It also works well when ran to a B-gap defensive tackle (3-technique). With no pullers the linebackers generally stay home and play their gaps.

VEER OPTION TO AN A-GAP DEFENSIVE TACKLE

Figure 110 shows Tex-Bone Veer Option to a 0 or 1-technique. The play side tackle is B-gap to play side linebacker. The play side guard is A-gap to the play side linebacker. One of these two players should be able to work up to the play side linebacker because both are rarely covered at the same time. The center is backside A-gap to backside linebacker, the backside guard is backside B-gap to backside linebacker, and the backside tackle covers the backside C-gap.

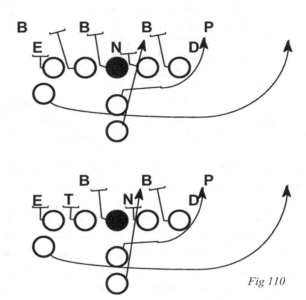

Fig 110

Tex-Bone Veer Option uses a straight gap blocking scheme comparable to a slide blocking pass protection. All offensive linemen first look for their immediate gap threat and a looping defensive lineman coming to them before moving to the linebacker.

The fullback in the two illustrations is again the dive player. (As he is in all triple option schemes.) Both illustrations show the wing from the backside as the pitch player. In the Tex-Bone there are many different ways to align or motion the pitch player. The quarterback keys the dive first, then the pitch key.

VEER OPTION TO A B-GAP DEFENSIVE TACKLE

The play side guard and play side tackle fold the 3-technique to the play side linebacker against a B-gap defensive tackle in the illustration on the next page. This is why the guard and tackle are described as "level one gap threat" to play side linebacker. One of these two players works to the play side linebacker regardless of the defensive front. It's more likely that the tackle works to the second level when running Veer Option to an A-gap defensive tackle. When running to a B-gap defensive tackle it is more likely that the guard works to level two.

We prefer to fold and wash down the 3-technique as the play side guard takes a skinny angle to the second level. Folding the 3-technique (see Figure 111) makes sense for three reasons:

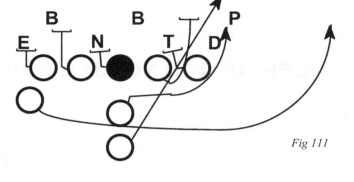

Fig 111

1.   Folding gives us a chance to wash the 3-technique laterally down level one to create space for the dive player.
2.   Folding around the back-blocking tackle gives the guard a better angle to reach the play side linebacker.
3.   There is a good chance the play side linebacker scrapes over the top of the guard and gets to the point of attack unhindered if we choose to send the guard directly to the second level. Folding gives the guard a better angle to the linebacker.

Veer option is the same on the backside against the B-gap as it is against an A-gap defensive tackle. The center, backside guard, and backside tackle are A-gap, B-gap, and C-gap.

The fullback needs to take a wider dive path to the B-gap because we are folding the 3-technique. This wider dive path requires a small amount of practice for the quarterback to learn where his first and second steps are so he reaches the mesh point with the fullback. The quarterback adjusts his first step to the inside leg of the guard (rather than his normal step to the outside foot of the center) in order to do so properly. This allows him to present the ball to the fullback on his wider B-gap path.

Nothing changes for the backside wing pitch player. Nothing changes for the quarterback's keys either. The quarterback reads the dive key first and the pitch key second.

VEER VS. THE BLITZ

Nothing changes against an edge blitz shown in Figure 112. (See the developing theme?) The dive key takes the fullback. The quarterback then anticipates the pitch defender containing the ball by covering the pitch back.

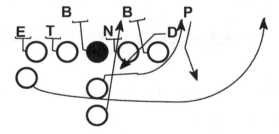

Defenses are not compelled to employ this type of blitz naturally. Defenses are able to assign the blitzing outside linebacker to the quarterback while the safety covers the pitch back. In most circumstances the pitch key (the blitzer) will take the pitch back and a safety will be responsible for the quarterback.

A key coaching point is making sure the tackle does not get engaged with the squeezing dive key. We want the tackle to work quickly to the play side linebacker.

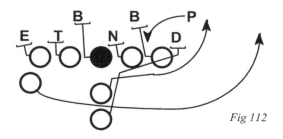

Fig 112

Expect to give the dive when facing a B-gap blitz because the dive key is working up field (see the bottom of Figure 112). The folding pitch key is likely to tackle the dive player in the hole on the give. This is why defenses blitz the B-gap.

Running a B-gap blitz is a big gamble for the defense however. Blitzing the pitch key to the B-gap is a great way to tackle dives but a bad way to cover pitches. The best counter is to block the dive key with the fullback (we call this a fullback load). The fullback load ensures that we get to the pitch phase of the play.

The chances for a big play increase when the fullback loads on the dive key, the pitch key spikes inside, and the ball gets pushed to the edge. Defenses take a large risk when they can't induce the dive give because the dive key is blocked. This means the pitch is insufficiently covered. The results are often large yardage gains.

POSITION FUNDAMENTALS

Fullback Fundamentals

We run our base A-gap dive against an A-gap defensive tackle. The dive path is to the B-gap against a B-gap defensive tackle. All paths are identical through the mesh point in the top illustration to the right. The dive player steps with his play side foot first before receiving the handoff with his inside elbow up.

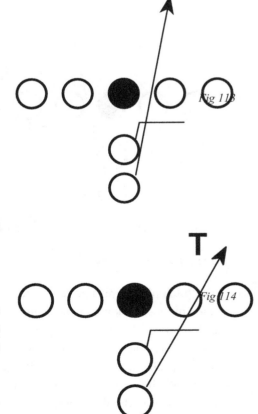

The dive must hit fast. Both the quarterback and fullback must work downhill quickly when the ball is snapped to maximize speed (see Figure 113). The level one read is the nearest defensive lineman down block. The level two read is the block on the play side linebacker.

Wide Fullback Path

Figure 114 shows the B-gap dive path. The quarterback must take his first step to the inside leg of the guard (instead of the outside leg of the center) to match the fullback. This is the dive path we prefer when running a play side fold block on a 3-technique.

Load Fullback Path

We discussed loading the fullback on the defensive end in the Power Option chapter. It's also a good choice when running the Veer Triple Option in the Tex-Bone. Figure 115 shows the fullback load.

Tight Fullback Path

Running a tight fullback path is also one of our options. We use the path (in Figure 116) when defensive ends attempt to give difficult looks to the quarterback (such as slow playing).

Sometimes defensive ends cross the line of scrimmage far enough to induce a give to the fullback. The defensive end then attempts to collapse inside and tackle the fullback after the give. Tightening the path of the dive player makes it increasingly difficult for the dive key to give unclear reads to the quarterback. This forces the dive key to move more decisively to either the dive player or the quarterback.

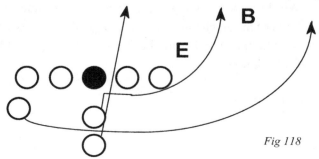

Fig 115

Quarterback Fundamentals

Quarterback fundamentals for Veer Option are the same as all triple option schemes. The first step is to the outside leg of the center while the second step squares the quarterback to path of the fullback as he dives to the A-gap. The

Fig 116

Quarterback then gives the ball to the dive player unless it is covered. It is the fullback's ball on Veer Option until the dive key forces the quarterback to take the ball from him. This is true with all triple option plays.

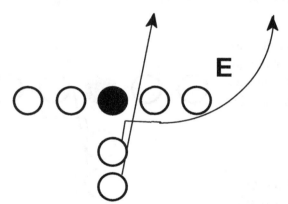

Fig 117

The quarterback in Figure 117 rides the fullback to his front foot in Veer Option. The QB must decide by the time the ball reaches his front foot whether he is giving to the fullback or pulling. He then attacks the alley if keeping the ball and enters the pitch phase.

Pitch Fundamentals

The pitch player must gain ground with his first step. Remember, the pitch player does not need motioning into pitch relationship as long as he moves efficiently at the snap. The pitch player aims for the quarterback's feet in Figure 118. The quarterback then steps downhill and out of the way with his first step. We want him to pass tightly behind the dive mesh on his way to pitch relationship (four to five yards). The pitch player

Fig 118

in the final phase gains width from the quarterback to receive the ball downhill toward the end zone.

Playside Wing/Slot Fundamentals

The slot or wing releases directly to the safety against the two high safety defenses in Figures 119 and 120. We cannot leave a safety unblocked to the play side.

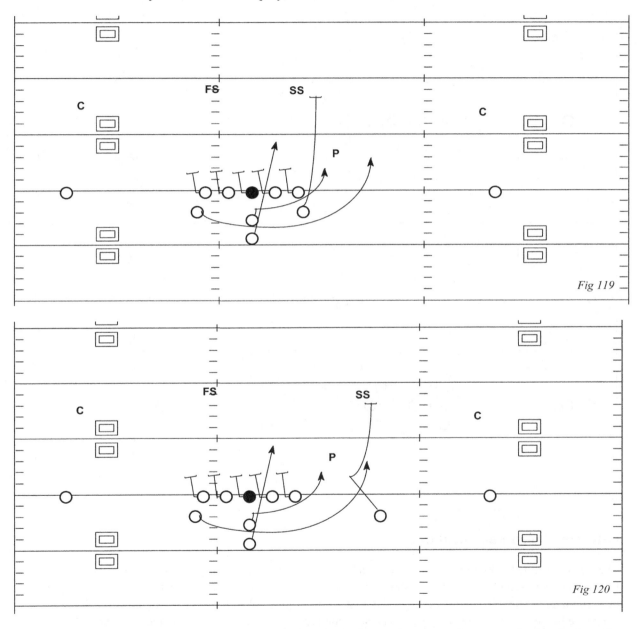

Fig 119

Fig 120

The wing or slot checks for scraping linebackers inside the box prior to moving towards the single safety against a one high safety defense. Illustrations 121 and 122 show these responsibilities.

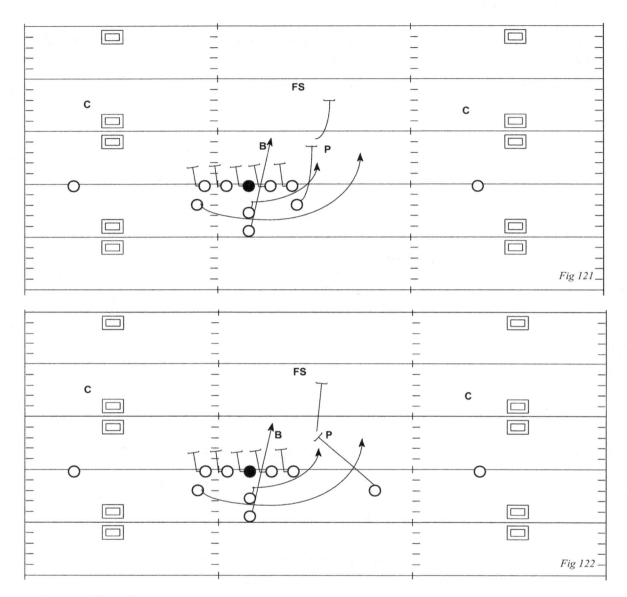

Fig 121

Fig 122

Offensive Line Fundamentals

The plays illustrated in Figure 123 features down blocks across the first level. Successful execution requires linemen to gain ground with their first step. The goal is to achieve horizontal displacement along the line of scrimmage. Blocking gap threats is the first rule of down blocking. Checking/blocking looping defensive linemen coming towards the gap is the second rule. Linemen then work to the near linebacker in the third phase.

Veer and Power differ in their blocking scheme. Front side blockers with no gap threat work to the play side linebacker in Veer. Front side blockers with no gap threat work to the backside linebacker in Power by contrast. This distinction is important for coaches and players to understand.

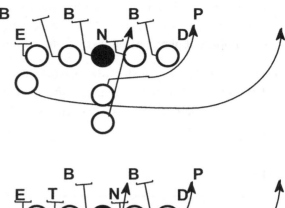

Linemen must anticipate linebacker movement once they process their responsibilities for the play (front side or backside linebackers). Anticipation is an essential component of successful blocking at the second level. A lineman stands to miss the block if he aims for where the linebacker is now instead of the linebacker's destination point.

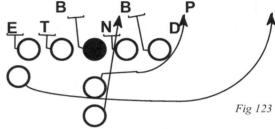

Fig 123

Play Side Tackle Arc Release

Arc releases (also described as a "banana" release) are an essential component of Veer Option.

Teams are likely to encounter squeeze and scrape defenses against the Veer. Squeeze and scrape means the defensive end squeezes down when the tackle releases inside and the play side linebacker scrapes over the top. The defensive end (who is the dive key) then takes the dive and the scraping linebacker takes the quarterback. This is a common tactic for combating Zone Read. It is also used against the Outside Veer.

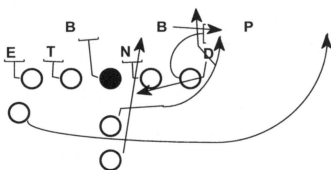

Fig 124

The tackle counters the squeeze and scrape by aiming for the linebacker scraping over the top. His path anticipates the linebacker's intended destination by taking an angle of intersection. The quarterback simultaneously anticipates the potential need to work underneath the offensive tackle on his way to the pitch phase.

Proper arc releases like the one in Figure 124 are an excellent response to squeeze and scrape defensive tactics.

Plays Blocked for Touchdowns

Triple option plays are blocked for touchdowns—not first downs. Most one-back plays in particular are not blocked for touchdowns because they often leave a safety unblocked. Play callers for triple option teams are able to match their offensive sets to the defense they are facing. This allows individualized blocking schemes to account for all play side defenders—including safeties.

Figures 125 and 126 show the blocking schemes for all interior players in Tex-Bone Veer. Naturally it is impossible to block every defender because one offensive player is running the ball. Our goal is to leave the unblocked player as far away from the point of attack as possible.

The play side wing or slot always works to the play side safety versus two high safety defenses in Figures 125 and 126. Chances of reaching the single high safety are still good after accounting for defenders in the box—including scraping linebackers in the second set of illustrations (Figures 127 and 128).

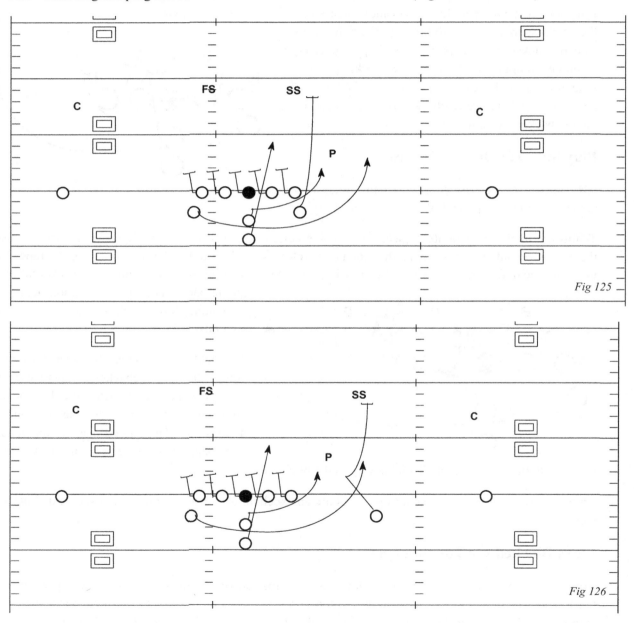

Fig 125

Fig 126

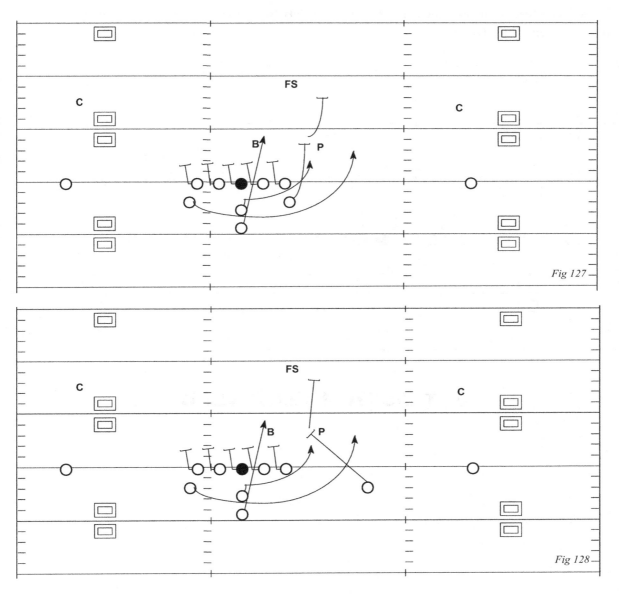

Fig 127

Fig 128

VEER READ

The Tex-Bone is able to run Veer Read in addition to the standard triple option Veer. The plays are similar beyond variances that distinguish the two blocking schemes. The dive key is the only player optioned in Veer Read. The quarterback gets the ball to the running back on the sweep if the dive key squeezes or pulls the ball and runs the dive path if the dive key works up field to contain the sweep player (see Figure 129).

We match our perimeter blocking to the defense presented. The Power Read chapter discusses several options for straight man-to-man blocking and cross blocking for the perimeter. Make sure your Power Read and Veer Read formations pick up the front side safety (or the only safety depending on the defense) at all times when game planning.

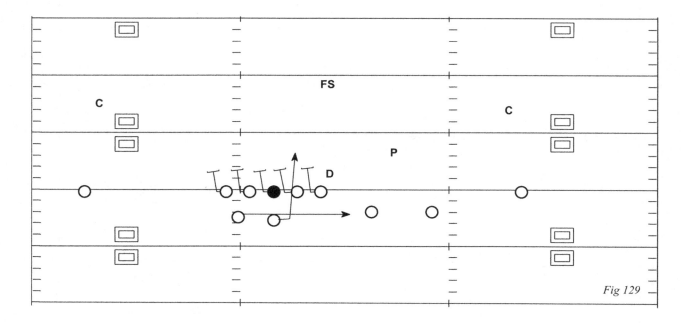

Fig 129

JET MOTION VEER READ

Jet Motion is another way to run Veer Read. Through Jet Motion we are able to run the sweep action with a motion player instead of with a stationary back. All the same rules from Jet Motion Power Read apply to Jet Motion Veer Read.

The back out of the backfield must arc release to the pitch key. The dive key is the only player being optioned. The front side wing or slot in the illustration on the previous page applies his one high safety or two high safety rules in terms of blocking responsibilities. (Figure 130 shows a one safety high defense specifically.)

Fig 130

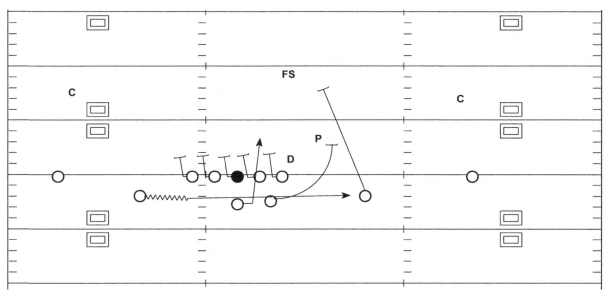

CHAPTER 11: ISOS & COUNTERS

ISOS & COUNTERS: the most versatile family in the Tex-Bone

Origins of the Lead Isolation Play

The Iso (short for Lead Isolation) is most closely associated with the "I" Formation. The "I" Formation is an adaptation of the "T" formation developed in the late 1940s at the Virginia Military Institute by head Coach Tom Nugent. Figure 131 shows running backs in the "Long I" used by Nugent instead of the traditional "T" formation.

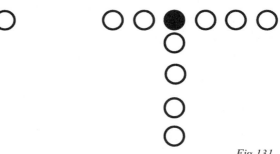

Fig 131

The modern "I" Formation became a favorite formation for NFL and college teams by the early 1960s. The Iso play (Figure 132) shows a downhill run that consistently yields positive yardage.

TEX-BONE ISOS

The Iso is the most versatile family of plays in the Tex-Bone. Isos offer opportunities for multiple lead blocker choices—including the center, guard, tackle, wing, or running back.

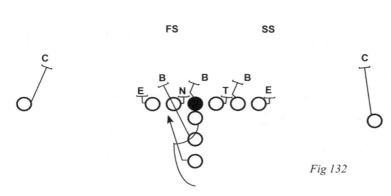

Fig 132

Benefits of Iso

Iso is a downhill, aggressive run scheme. While not blocked for a touchdown, it is blocked for first downs and blocked for consistent yardage gains. Iso plays are available from multiple formations and with multiple ball carriers. Because of its aggressive nature the Iso should yield few negative plays.

Flexbone Iso

The Flexbone Iso uses the play side wing as the Iso blocker. This puts the lead blocker one-on-one with the play side linebacker at the point of attack. All other players on the front side are man-to-man. The tackle is man-to-man on the defensive end and the guard is man-to-man on the nose tackle in the top of Figure 133.

The tackle is man-to-man on the defensive end and the guard is man-to-man on the 3-technique defensive tackle in bottom of Figure 133. The lead Isolation player works to the play side linebacker in the open gap. The wing then adjusts and works through the appropriate open gap if defensive linemen move and the open gap shifts.

All offensive linemen block gaps on the backside of the Iso. The center blocks the A-gap, the guard is on B-gap, and the tackle is on C-gap. The fullback runs an A or B-gap dive path depending on where the open gap is. The quarterback's footwork then matches the fullback's path.

Fig 133

Flexbone Iso vs. Blitz

Flexbone Iso is doable against the blitz—even though it's not a preferable choice.

The play side wing (or Iso blocker) must adapt to wherever the blitz is coming from and neutralize it. Figure 134 shows play side blitzes. The play side wing vacates his Isolation of the play side linebacker and blocks

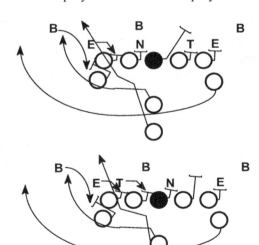

the immediate threat off the edge (or C-gap) in response to the blitz. This is not an ideal play against defensive pressure because it leaves the inside linebacker free. The play should still gain yardage before the linebacker tackles the fullback however.

There are times when teams get caught by a blitz when running Iso. A quarterback is best served to change the play to Speed Option if the correct pre-snap blitz read is made. This is the built-in advantage of running the Flexbone triple option—it dissuades blitzes.

Fig 134

Flexbone Iso Option

Few things change when the Flexbone Iso becomes Flexbone Option as shown in Figure 135. The first noteworthy difference is the fullback midline dive path illustrated in the two plays on the next page. This path gives the fullback a chance to work inside-out past the play side linebacker to the third level.

The wing still Isos the play side linebacker. Off the token fake the quarterback knows he is pulling the ball and attempting to work around the edge to the pitch phase. Nothing else changes in the blocking scheme beyond those considerations.

Flexbone Iso Option vs. Blitz

Flexbone Iso Option is a better choice against the blitz than a straight Flexbone Iso. The offense gains an advantage by optioning the blitzing linebacker instead of relying on the play side wing to pick up the blitz. Nothing else changes with the blocking scheme. The play side wing works to the play side linebacker through the open gap.

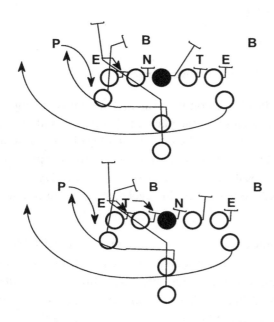

Fig 135

Fig 136

Figure 136 shows the C-gap open with the play side tackle man-to-man on the defensive end. The offensive tackle must follow the defensive end spiking inside and the play side wing adjusts to find the open gap in order to get to his linebacker.

The token fake to the fullback follows the midline path before attempting to sort through the moving players in front of him to reach the third level of the defense. The quarterback and backside wing then option the blitzing pitch key.

The quarterback is always well served to check into speed option if unsure about the reliability of the scheme based on the defensive pre-snap read. Speed option is always good against any front. It is a reliable safety blanket for the quarterback.

Spread Center Iso

Play callers get the advantage of choosing what player to use as lead isolation blockers. A pulling lineman becomes the lead Isolation blocker for plays illustrated on the next page. Either the center or the guard pulls. Let's start by analyzing Spread Center Iso diagrams.

Center and Guard Isos are designed to capitalize on five man boxes with zone coverage behind it. This is either an odd front five-man box (bottom of Figure 137) or an even front five-man box (top of Figure 137).

Center Iso features man-to-man blocking on the front side by the play side tackle and the play side guard while the backside uses modified zone blocking. The center pulls around as the Iso blocker aiming for the single linebacker in the box instead of inserting the wing like in earlier Flexbone Isos.

The same rules apply to blocking 3-2 box defenses in the bottom illustration to the right. The play side tackle is man-to-man on the defensive end, the play side guard is man-to-man on the nose tackle, and the center pulls to the play side linebacker while the guard and tackle are two-for-two on the backside.

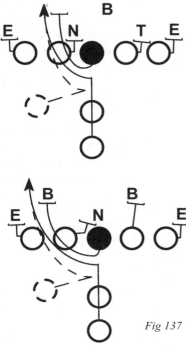

This scheme is available with a fullback alignment (the fullback behind the quarterback) and a running back alignment (the back offset to the side of the quarterback). We prefer to align our offset back toward the puller when running Iso. The play promotes hesitation or false movement from the isolated linebacker by meshing towards the pull. This mesh point makes the Iso gap larger and more accessible to the puller and the ball carrier.

Teams are limited to running Center Iso toward the A-gap defensive tackle out of spread. This means running the play towards a 0, 1 or 2-technique.

Spread Guard Iso

Fig 137

You are not limited in direction when running Spread Guard Iso however. (Running to an A-gap or B-gap defensive tackle are available choices). Both the Guard and Center Isos are designed to capitalize on a five-man box with zone coverage behind it.

The rules for Guard Iso are the same for Center Iso. Both the play side tackle and guard are blocking man-to-man. This leaves the center and backside tackle to account for the last two defenders while the backside guard makes the pull. The center in Figure 138 executes a back block to cover for the pulling guard. This scheme is similar to the back block on Power. Guard Iso is available from either a fullback or running back alignment.

Center/Guard Iso Considerations

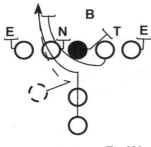

Fig 138

There are several considerations worth taking into account when running Center and Guard Isos:

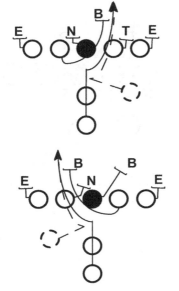

1. The quarterback must identify man coverage and get to Speed Option if facing pressure. These are five-man

box plays not designed to attack pressure looks.

2.   Pull your best players. Some players are better at base blocking and some players are better at pulling. Choose the scheme that fits your personnel. Run Center Iso if your best puller is the center and Guard Iso if the best puller is the guard.

3.   Center Iso is particularly good at neutralizing guard keys. Few teams key the center pull as part of their defensive strategy. Pull the center if you want to limit guard reactions.

4.   Compliment this by selecting backfield actions that mimic other players or induce beneficial linebacker reactions away from the point of attack.

5.   Create a six-man box response. A plan including a Tackle Iso is good if you want to stay with an Iso scheme. Changing the play to Speed Option is always a good choice.

6.   Teams must pull the center to the open B-gap "bubble." The "bubble" refers to the open area between the nose tackle and defensive end. ("I" Formation Iso coaches are already familiar with the term.)

7.   Pulling to any surface (including to or away from the "bubble") is an option when pulling the guard. It does not matter what gap is open when pulling the guard on an Iso.

QB Iso

QB Iso is one of my favorite plays because it's an aggressive, fast hitting, downhill play. The aggressiveness of QB Iso sneaks up on teams that expect laterally moving triple option plays.

The quarterback Iso is a running back lead play. He aligns to the side of the quarterback and attacks the play side linebacker. Teams are able to run this play to any surface and open gap. The three plays in Figure 139 show QB Iso.

Coaching point: the running back must get the ball behind him in order to create a favorable inside-out blocking angle. The running back is not running directly at the play side linebacker. The linebacker might cross his face and reach the quarterback unabated if the running back did this. This is why the running back must get the ball behind him and then work inside-out to the outside number.

The quarterback takes two steps to the opposite A-gap on QB Iso. This counter action holds the backside

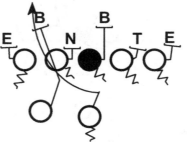

linebacker and sets up a beneficial blocking angle for the running back on the play side linebacker. The misdirection aspect of the play is an important component in large yardage gains.

QB Iso turns into QB Draw when ran with pass sets. Linemen show pass influence to sell the play. The running back then slow plays his approach the play side linebacker to mimic the

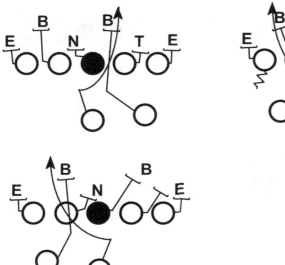

Fig 139

demeanor of pass protection. Linemen still follow Iso rules even though they give ground to sell pass to the defense.

COUNTERS

Counters are considered a part of the Iso family in the Tex-Bone. The following sections detail their place in the offense.

Spread Tackle Iso

Spread Tackle Isos are some of our favorite spread run plays. Pulling the center or guard to run an Iso with five defenders in the box was discussed in previous sections. Pulling a tackle allows you to account for six defenders in the box.

Tackle Iso also provides the opportunity to incorporate counter backfield actions. Front side blockers are man-to-man in all Iso plays. Figure 140 shows the tackle and guard on the play side blocking man-to-man with the center and guard playing zone and accounting for the A-gap and B-gap on the backside. The tackle then pulls through the open gap to the front side linebacker.

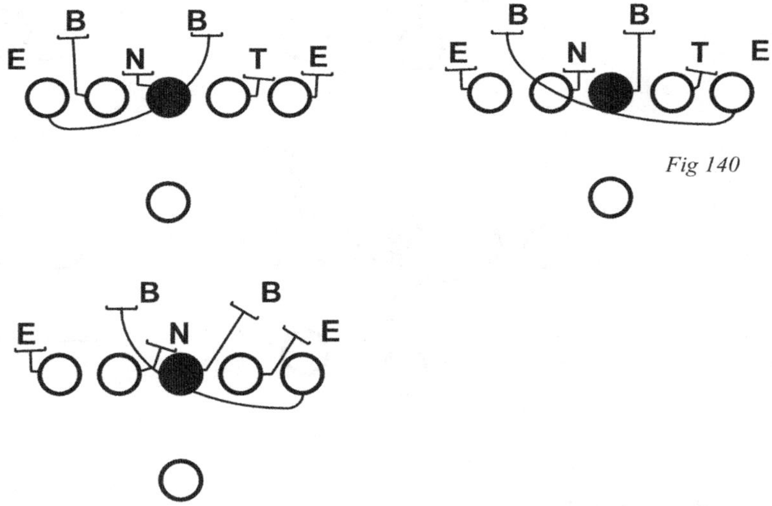

Fig 140

Adding a tight end to the backside helps eliminate the backside read. The tight end secures the C-gap and (in most cases) counters any sort of blitz situation.

The backside defensive end is potentially unblocked without a tight end. The defensive end needs accounting for by reading (optioning) him or blocking him with some other player.

Tackle Iso Backfield Actions

There are four actions that pair well with Tackle Iso:

1. Dive counter (top left of Figure 141): off the dive mesh the running back bows out slightly to follow the tackle through the open gap. The quarterback must key the backside defensive end and keep the ball if the defensive end is going to tackle the running back.
2. Speed Option counter (top right of Figure 141): on the Speed Option counter the running back takes off laterally for three hard steps. He turns back on his third step to the inside and receives the ball from quarterback. The quarterback must position himself slightly behind the running back to mesh effectively. It's his job to press the edge quickly and get

the ball to the running back right as he pivots back to the play. Speed Option counter creates a lot of influence with the linebackers even if it is slow developing at the snap. The quarterback must key the backside defensive end and keep the ball if he is going to tackle the running back.

3. Quarterback counter (bottom left of Figure 141): this play features a dive mesh with the running back peeling off and blocking the backside end after the fake. Remember, without a tight end the backside defensive end needs accounting for. Using the running back to block the backside defensive end is one possibility on QB counter.

4. Fullback counter (bottom right of Figure 141): The fourth backfield choice is to run Tackle Iso with a fullback setting up the dive path away from the Iso before bending back to the play side and following the tackle.

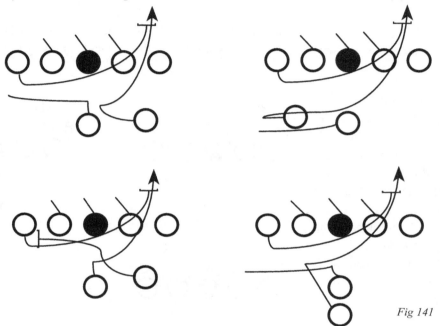

Fig 141

Spread Tackle Iso vs. Blitz

Defensive pressure should not adversely affect Tackle Iso. This is true because all gaps are accounted for. The pulling tackle accounts for the C-gap edge rusher on the blitz (see Figure 142). This essentially becomes a C-gap Iso for the tackle. The play becomes an A-gap Iso if the defense commits an A-gap blitzer.

The guard and tackle are always man-to-man on the near defensive tackle and defensive end. The pulling tackle then fits to the open gap based on the blitz. The man-to-man side stays man-to-man and the backside blockers are still A-gap and B-gap.

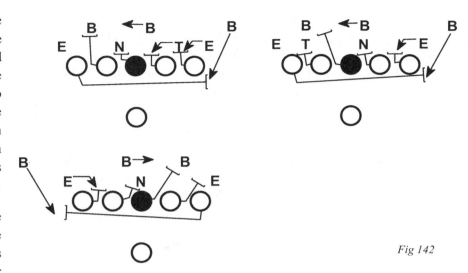

Fig 142

The unblocked inside linebacker in the illustrations to the right is held by the counter backfill action. Remember, our Tackle Isos are all counter plays. There is always misdirection working away from where the tackle is pulling to. Backfield action should pull the unblocked inside linebacker away from the point of attack.

Pre-snap communication is particularly important because the backside puller needs to know if a blitz is coming and what gap he needs to cover (either is A-gap, B-gap, or C-gap). It's also important for the quarterback to identify blitz keys so the guard and tackle make adjustments for any slanting defensive players.

The unchanging nature of Iso rules helps teams cope with pressure. Practice also assuages the blitzes that defenses apply from week to week. Quarterbacks quickly learn to audible into Speed Option if players are struggling with adjusting at the line of scrimmage.

G-T Counter

The Tex-Bone also uses the G-T Counter. It is a hybrid combination of Power and Tackle Iso concepts. The following sections detail how it works.

Evolution of the G-T Counter

Early versions of the G-T Counter date back to the Wing T. The Tex-Bone G-T Counter is a combination of Power and Tackle Iso. The play utilizes two lead blockers as pullers from the backside with down blocks on the front side.

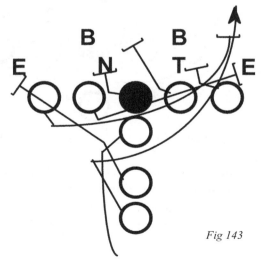

Fig 143

The University of Nebraska was the first college team to use the G-T Counter from the "I" Formation under Coach Tom Osborne. Their success with the "I" Formation G-T Counter made the play popular across all levels of football. The play became the calling card of the Washington Redskins under head coach Joe Gibbs. The Redskins used this play in Figure 143 into the 1990s.

The term "Counter" eventually became synonymous with any two players from the backside pulling to the front side. Figure 144 shows an example of H-Back Counter. Notice the backside guard pull to the contain player and the H-Back pull to the play side linebacker in the illustration. This blocking scheme is frequently paired with run pass options in recent years.

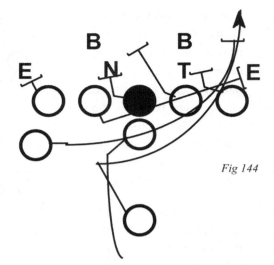

Fig 144

Tex-Bone G-T Counter

The G-T Counter in the Tex-Bone offense is nothing more than a combination of Power and Tackle Iso (see Figure

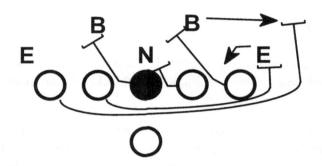

145). We like G-T Counter because it adds versatility and misdirection choices to the Tex-Bone spread playbook. We like to run G-T Counter as a Counter Read play and we also run G-T Counter with Jet Motion.

The backside guard pulls while the front side players down block. The G-T Counter and Power blocking schemes are the same in this regard. The backside tackle then pulls and Isos just as he does on Tackle Iso. These blocking rules are highly effective and do not require players to learn an entirely new blocking scheme in order to run G-T Counter.

We always want to log block. The pulling guard always pulls with the intent of logging. He then reacts accordingly if a kick out is required. The pulling backside tackle works outside the log on his way to the play side linebacker (assuming a

Fig 145

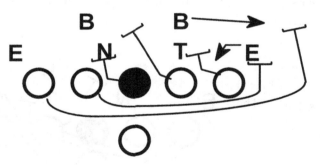

log block is available—a kick out is used if not).

Figure 146 shows kick out blocking against odd and even man fronts. The pulling guard is forced to kick out if the defensive end works too far up field for log blocking. The pulling tackle then makes an adjustment by pulling up inside of the kick out in order to reach the play side linebacker. The ball carrier sees the new path and adjusts to match his block.

G-T Counter Backfield Actions

We like to run G-T Counter with Jet Motion. We already examined a few different blocking schemes for Jet Motion in previous sections.

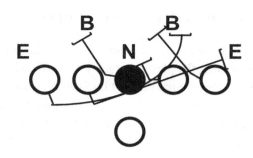

With Jet Motion the play is somewhat unique in that there is no read. The quarterback must remain patient on the fake to help the counter action develop however. Any need for a read on Jet Motion is eliminated with the running back block of the contain player. The Jet Motion in the top part of Figure 147 goes away from the counter block. This movement away from the play side negates the need for a counter read.

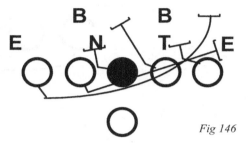

We also run G-T Counter with a read (bottom portion of Figure 147). This is known as "Bash" in many spread circles. We run this by bringing the running back across the face the quarterback on a sweep path. The quarterback gives the ball to the running back if the defensive end doesn't take away the sweep. Pulling the ball and following the counter blocking is the best decision when the defensive end works up field to cover the sweep.

Fig 146

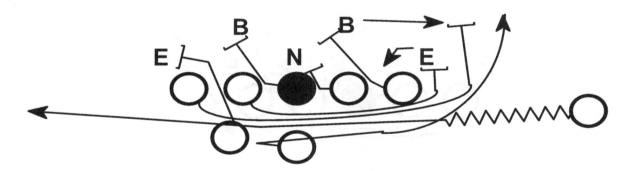

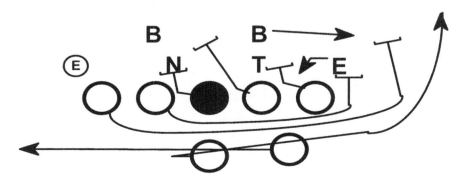

Fig 147

Spread G-T Counter vs. Blitz

G-T Counter (like Power) is good against pressure. The only change (similar to one-back Power Read) is assigning the play side tackle to block man-to-man on the play side defensive end. This allows the pulling guard to take the blitzing linebacker while the pulling tackle works inside to kick out to isolate the play side linebacker (see Figure 148). Failure to identify the blitz leads to a poor numbers situation. Identifying the blitz transforms the G-T Counter into a good play call against pressure.

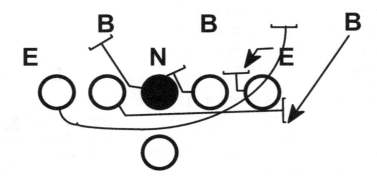

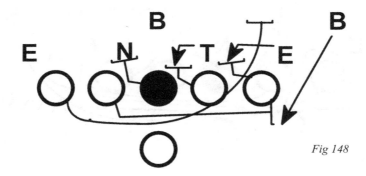

Fig 148

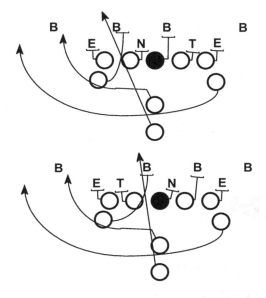

PASS GAME

12. **Power Option Pass**

13. **G Load Pass**

14. **Double Pull Power Pass**

15. **Power Read Pass**

16. **Iso Pass**

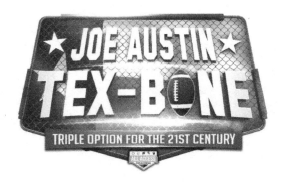

105

CHAPTER 12: POWER OPTION PASS

POWER OPTION PROTECTION

Power Option Protection looks identical to Power Option Run with the pulling guard taking the play side C-gap (edge) and the fullback blocking the play side linebacker. All other assignments are identical to Power Run otherwise.

Figure 149 shows how Power Option Protection looks like its running counterpart up to the point where the pulling guard clears the play side guard. The pulling guard in Power Option Protection continues flat down the line of scrimmage to block the C-gap defender instead of turning up field (like in a Power run).

The complete picture of the play side looks like this: the guard takes the A-gap, the tackle takes the B-gap, and the pulling guard takes the C-gap.

The fullback blocks the play side linebacker in Power Option Protection. There's a high probability the play side linebacker is filling on the play. There's also a high probability the backside linebacker is scraping because the backside gap is removed by the play side guard pull. The backside linebacker then gains the potential of joining the pass rush. This rush is delayed if the linebacker is scraping however. The uncovered play side guard or tackle gets an opportunity to pick up this delayed rusher coming from the backside.

Coaching point: remember that everything in Power Option Protection looks just like Power Run. The quarterback does everything the exact same. The demeanor of the offensive line is the exact same. The fullback's path through the mesh is identical to the run—even though his job is now pass blocking.

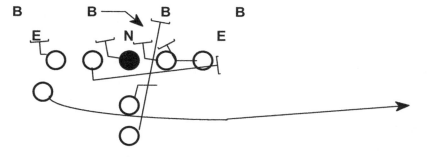

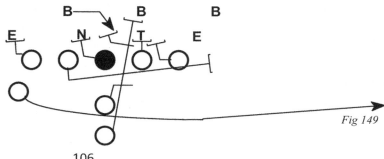

Fig 149

106

Power Option Protection vs. Blitz

The only thing that changes against a blitz is the quarterback assigns the play side tackle to block the defensive end man-to-man. This allows the pulling guard to account for any blitzing defender—whether it comes to the B or C-gap.

The play side linebacker is still accounted for by the fullback. The backside wing (normally working over the top of the quarterback to get into a pass pattern) must vacate the option fake to stay home and protect the backside edge. In Figure 150 the wing comes off his option path and secures the backside edge if he feels there is a backside threat on the play—even if he already started into his option path. His job is to work inside to establish leverage against the outside blitz wherever it appears.

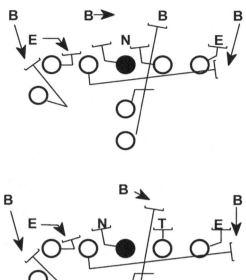

Fig 150

SHORT & INTERMEDIATE PASS PROTECTION & ROUTE COMBOS

All of the pass plays in the following sections are available with a variety of formations, protections, and backfield actions. Our examination looks at these pass plays from 2x1 Spread formations with a wing aligned to the weak side. The 2x1 Spread formation serves as a common Tex-Bone formation example.

Flood

There's nothing magical about the Tex-Bone Flood—it is the same as all other Flood passes in football. The Flood in Figure 151 is a three-level pass play. There's always a deep stretch (in this case by the outside split end). There is also an intermediate-level out route by the slot receiver. The slot receiver gets the most beneficial play-action influence by stemming inside as if he is blocking the linebacker or getting leverage to block the safety. After this stem he stretches vertically to 10 yards before bending his out route to 12 yards. The flat stretch comes from the backside wing coming over the top of the quarterback as if he's the pitch player. Rather than turning up to receive a pitch he continues to stretch into the flat.

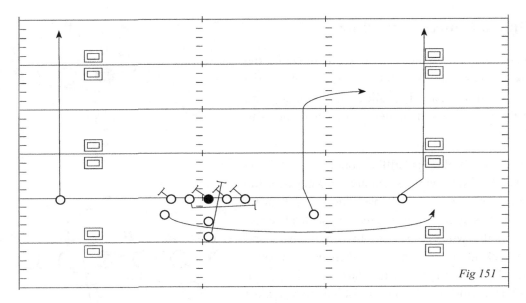

Fig 151

Flood is intended to take deep coverage vertical. This sets up a two-on-one advantage against the curl-to flat-defender.

The purpose of the run action is to get pass defenders (such as the curl defender) to trigger on the run. The ball is then easily delivered to the out route for a sizeable gain when the defender exposes the curl zone.

Quick Flood

A cousin of the Flood pass is the Quick Flood pass. The Quick Flood creates a similar stretch—only the play develops quicker. The Quick Flood requires a change in terms of the defender the quarterback reads. The corner is read in this case instead of the curl defender.

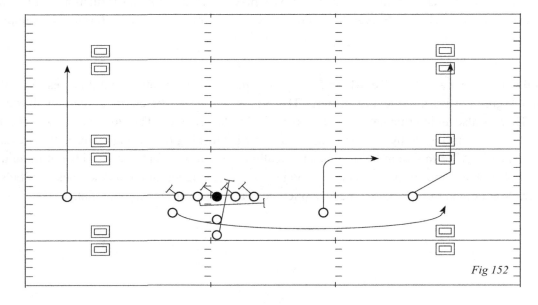

Fig 152

The outside vertical release and the quick out route in Figure 152 create a fast developing high-low on the corner. The ball goes to the out route if the corner commits to the vertical release. The vertical down the sideline then opens up if the corner sits in the flat and covers the out route.

The wing works over the top of the backfield into the flat as a third option if the high-low on the corner fails to develop. Coaching note: the throw to the out route in the flat is a quick decision—not a last second dump off.

Dig

The next Power Option Pass is the Dig. Our outside split end runs the Dig route in the Tex-Bone. This route is a Speed Dig rather than a traditional post-dig. Figure 153 shows the receiver pressing his route stem to 10 yards before rounding inside at about 12 yards. The inside wide receiver presses vertically fast enough to entice the deep coverage to carry him down the field. Underneath the flat stretch comes from the backside wing. This wing works over the top of the quarterback to the flat if he is not needed in pass protection.

The Dig is a curl/flat read working the opposite of Flood. A deep vertical stretch inside still pulls the coverage, a route still enters the curl zone at 12 yards, and a wing still stretches to the flat.

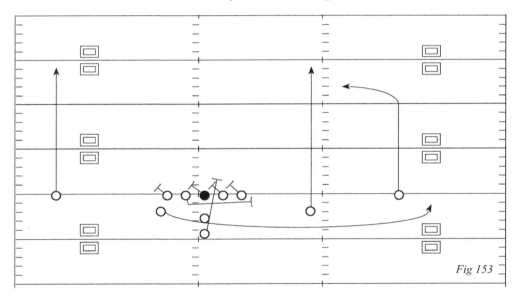

Fig 153

The objective of the Dig is to put the curl-to-flat defender in a situation where he cannot cover all the space assigned to him. Ideally a curl defender triggers at the snap to cover Power Option Run—leaving the curl and flat zone vacated. Zone defenders that trigger to the run cannot cover passes effectively. Any delay in the defensive back read provides an advantage.

Quick Dig

The Quick Dig is a nice compliment to the Speed Dig. It resembles the Speed Dig, only quicker (at a more shallow depth—five yards instead of 12). We look for the same vertical stretch by the slot receiver. The outside quick dig opens up if the curl defender covers the inside vertical or triggers toward the line of scrimmage to cover the run.

Figure 154 shows an opportunity to hit the vertical seam as it passes through the curl zone if the outside linebacker triggers to cover the Power Option run play and vacates the curl zone all together. We consider the vertical pattern passing through the curl zone the "curl route" and the quick dig is considered the "flat route."

The wing working on top is a check down option if the play goes sideways. In most cases the ball goes to the vertical seam or the quick dig before the wing gets to the flat however.

We want the throw predicated on the initial movement of the curl/flat defender. The seam route is our first read/look. The second option is the Quick Dig. The third option is the wing in the flat.

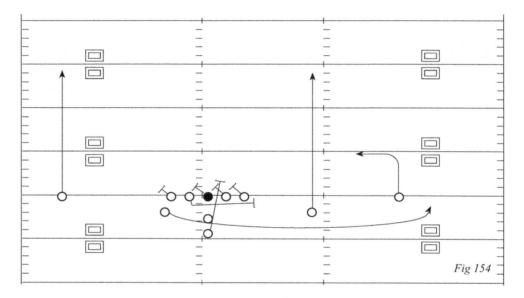

Fig 154

Backside Isolations

Single receiver routes are something we tag frequently. Figure 155 shows how various routes in the Tex-Bone system look as a single-receiver isolation. In-breaking routes including stop routes, slants, digs, or posts are available to the inside. Out-breaking routes including quick outs, deep outs, and post corners are also available.

We look to tag these routes when there is no safety helping the corner on the backside of the play. One-on-one situations with no safety help are great opportunities to tag a single wide receiver route.

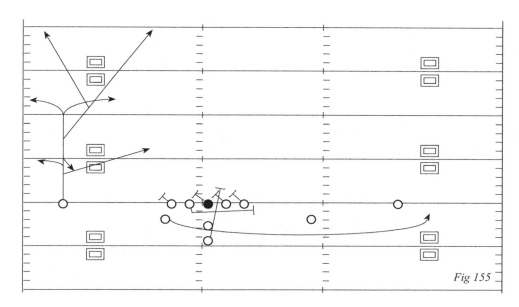

Fig 155

Downfield Shots

Downfield shots are pre-built into the Tex-Bone system. We select the ones that best fit our needs when game planning for an upcoming opponent. One of our favorite built-in downfield shots is the Double Post. Figure 156 shows how the Double Post to the play side sets up a variety of options based on coverage.

The quarterback looks to the double post side against any two high safety defenses. Against a half-field safety to the double post side the quarterback looks to high-low the safety with the Double Post. The Double Post essentially turns into two man-to-man post routes against quarters coverage. The quarterback then throws to the better of the two man-to-man matchups.

The Double Post combo is not a good choice against a single high safety because the inside post is covered by the free safety in the middle and the outside post is covered by the corner in the deep third. In situations like this we look to target the backside post-corner. Our intent is to leverage the corner inside on the post move and beat him to the edge of the field on the corner move.

The wing stretching to the flat is a suitable check-down if downfield reads do not develop. This check-down is available against any coverage.

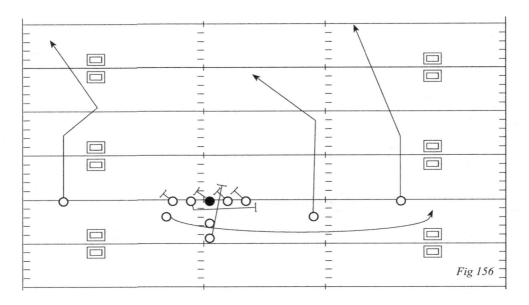

Fig 156

ADDITIONAL BACKFIELD ACTIONS

A valuable Tex-Bone element is the ability to use Power Option runs and Power Option passes from a variety of formations and multiple backfield actions. Chapter 1 detailed twelve ways to accomplish this in the run game. The previous pages showed several different passing combinations in the Tex-Bone.

Starting in 2x2 Open with motion from slot to a wing is one example of how formations and movement are used to get players into the desired alignment. Figure 157 shows this by starting in 2x2 Open and motioning the slot receiver down to the wing position.

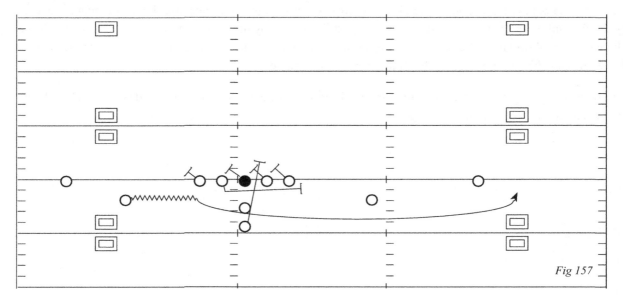

Fig 157

Operating from a 2x1 Open formation with a wing on the strong side is also an option. Figure 158 shows how the wing (1) enters the pitch phase of a run play or (2) becomes a check down receiver. Note how starting the wing from the strong side does not hinder his execution of responsibilities on the play.

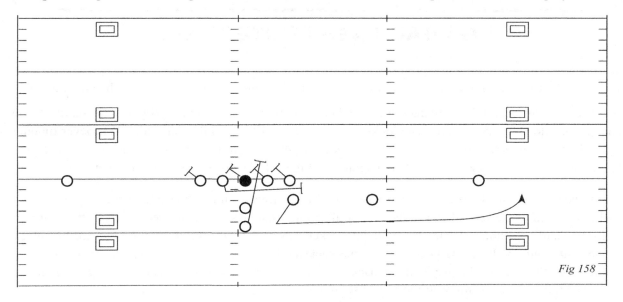

Fig 158

There are a multitude of pass options in the Tex-Bone system. The formation and personnel options are only limited by your imagination.

CHAPTER 13: G LOAD PASSES

G LOAD PASS PROTECTION

G Load Pass Protection looks identical to G Load run. Everything mirrors the run scheme on the play side in particular. The fold combination comes between the play side tackle and play side guard. If the play side tackle faces no gap threat he looks for a linebacker filling on the play side. Whenever running any G Load scheme we pull with the intent of logging the contain player. The guard reacts when the defensive end forces a kick out. The two diagrams of Figure 159 show G Load Pass Protection.

The primary difference between G Load Pass and G Load Run is on the backside of the play we do not work downfield to the second level. The bottom illustrations shows the uncovered linemen (the center or backside guard) accounting for the backside linebacker. Essentially this protection is a two-for-two block by the center and the backside guard against the backside linebacker and the nearest defensive lineman. The fullback then blocks the play side linebacker off the dive fake. This linebacker is likely filling to the play. The fullback meets him near the line of scrimmage.

The quarterback presses the fake along the line of scrimmage after the dive mesh occurs. Most of the routes we pair with G Load Pass Protection allow the quarterback to press the fake a significant distance along the line of scrimmage before setting up to deliver the pass. The quarterback's ability to press the fake laterally greatly enhances the play-action influence of this protection. His lateral press puts greater pressure on outside linebackers.

If the quarterback keeps the ball outside the pocket it forces outside linebackers to fill and vacate their pass zones. This action induces similar reactions by safeties with primary run support duties (safeties in Cover 4 schemes specifically).

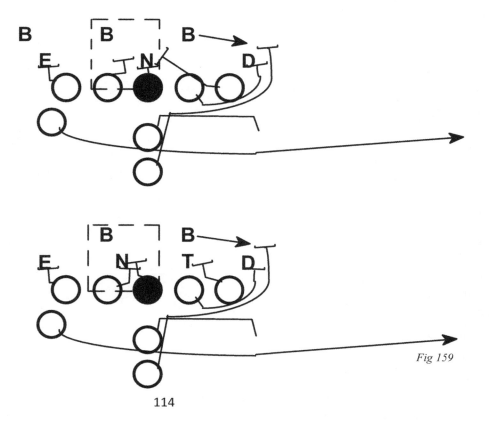

Fig 159

114

G Load Pass Protection vs. Blitz

G Load Pass Protection accounts for pressure situations effectively. Figure 160 demonstrates how the protection accounts for a linebacker blitzing off the edge. This is achieved through blitz awareness/pickup with the fullback. The protection is virtually unchanged for all other players against the blitz.

The guard and tackle fold block versus an edge blitz actually becomes easier in this case. The dive key usually works down to the B-gap against an edge blitzer. This creates an easy log block for the pulling guard. The play side tackle stays with the 3-technique slanting inside to the A-gap.

Against an edge blitz on the backside there are three players to block three gaps. The center, guard, and tackle protect the A-gap, B-gap, and C-gap respectively.

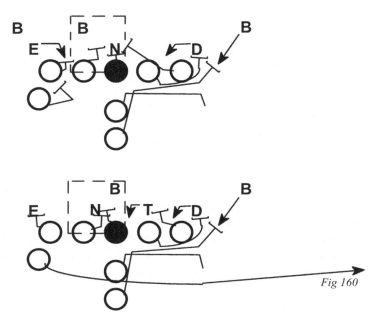

Fig 160

INTERMEDIATE &

DEEP ROUTES

G Load pass plays push the ball downfield in search of large gains. The following sections detail how receivers get into the right position to maximize big play potential.

Base Blocks & Vertical Releases

The most effective way to push the ball downfield is to sell the base block before releasing into a vertical route. Play side receivers start by releasing as if they are blocking the safety and corner before getting vertical.

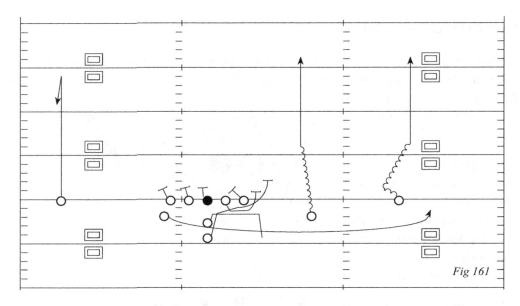

Fig 161

Figure 161 shows the play side outside receivers releasing vertically and stacking over the top when the safety and corner fill to cover the run. On the backside of the play we tag a timing route so the quarterback knows where to deliver the ball safely versus man coverage. (G Load Pass builds in a timing route to account for blitzes and other situations when vertical routes are not open).

While there are a number of backside timing route choices the one we use most frequently is a comeback. Check down options for the quarterback also includes the flat stretch if neither the corner nor safety fills to cover the run.

An important aspect of selling the run on G Load Pass plays is the quarterback pressing the fake toward the edge of the defense. Our G Load Pass Protection routes typically take longer to develop than our Power Option Pass routes. Selling the fake to the edge helps hold defenders long enough for pass routes to get open in space.

Cross Blocks & Vertical Releases

Cross blocks with vertical releases are another combination well suited for pushing the ball downfield. As show in Figure 162, cross blocks create an advantage in terms of blocking leverage and timing when blocks are made in relation to when the ball arrives at the point of attack (cross blocks are extremely effective at selling the run before becoming a pass). Cross blocking is the best method for engaging outside defenders as the ball arrives at the point of attack.

It's logical for the Tex-Bone to place high emphasis on cross block play-action pass routes because Tex-Bone run plays throughout the entire offense employ cross blocks on the outside.

Big plays in the pass game often come from cross blocks and vertical releases. A downfield void is left in the space a defender vacates when the corner or safety fills downhill to cover the run. This void becomes the point of exploitation.

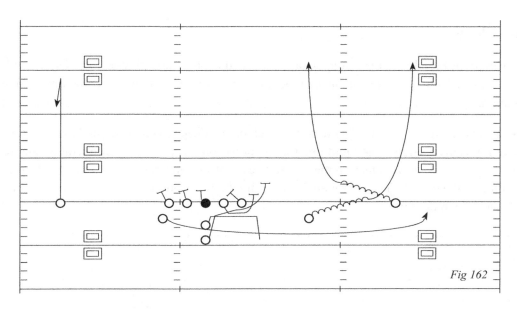

Fig 162

Crack Block & Vertical Releases

Crack blocks that transition into vertical releases are highly effective as well. We often crack block our split end and leave the corner as the pitch player when running triple option to the boundary. This action creates a tremendous play-action opportunity.

Figure 163 shows the play side split end crack blocking before releasing vertically up field. In execution he patiently releases inside to sell a run block on the safety. The split end releases vertically into the vacated area when the safety fills to cover the triple option run.

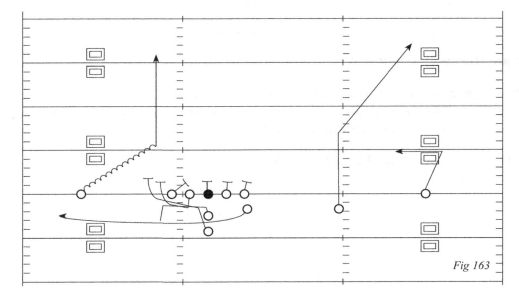

Fig 163

Tight End Flood

There are a variety of Flood patterns available out of G Load triple option play-action. Tight End Flood in particular is highly effective. More than just a Flood, this is an opportunity to target the tight end in a one-on-one situation.

Figure 164 shows the Tight End releasing to sell a block on the deep coverage aligned over the top of him. This defender is usually a safety. The Tight End runs a corner route when the deep coverage squeezes down to fill the run. In a check down situation the quarterback looks to underneath routes if the deep coverage does not commit to the run fill. The near wing is generally the first option and the backside wing is usually the second check down option.

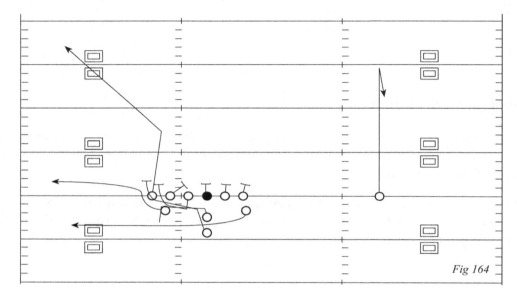

Fig 164

Single Wide Receiver Isolations

G Load Pass Protection also provides the opportunity for single wide receiver isolations. These opportunities are available from a variety of formations. The next two illustrations show single wide receiver isolations out of the Shotgun Flexbone formation.

Figure 165 tags a post route to the G Load Pass Protection.

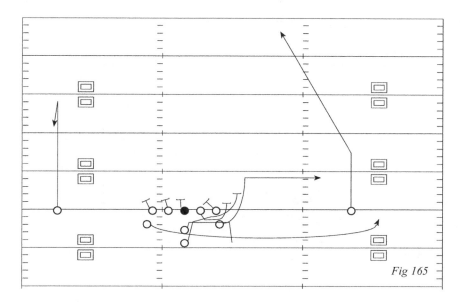

Fig 165

The natural complement in Figure 166 is the outside receiver running a post-corner route.

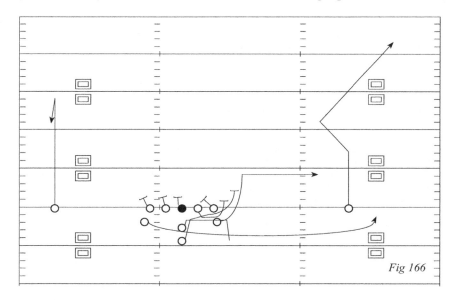

Fig 166

Timing and man-to-man pass patterns are also built in to single receiver isolations. We like to run timing routes on the backside of pass plays that let the quarterback know where to throw if he doesn't like his front side options. This route is often a 14-yard comeback for.

There are many other good route choices too. Standard check down options are automatically built into the play. Both the front and backside wings are available if the man-to-man isolation route does not develop.

We also like using stop routes as play side timing routes. Stops effectively build in the complimentary stop-and-go and double stop-and-go routes shown in the next Figure (167). G Load Option Pass Protection typically affords ample time to support double move routes. This additional time is achieved by using a six-man pass protection scheme with a quarterback stretch along the line of scrimmage.

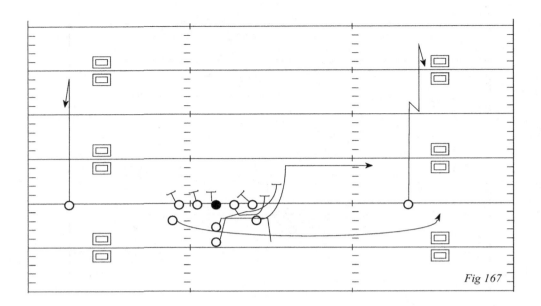

Fig 167

CHAPTER 14: DOUBLE PULL POWER PASS

DOUBLE PULL POWER PASS: seven and eight man protection with five receiver patterns or single receiver isolations

Double Pull Power Protection

Double Pull Power pass protection looks identical to Double Pull Power run blocking. Both the run and pass variants provide seven or eight-man protection with blitz pick up built in. Double Pull Power pass protection also supports five receiver patterns or single receiver isolations.

Figure 168 shows the Double Pull Power Protection. In all Tex-Bone play-action passes we want the play to look the same as a run. An important aspect in this sell is that all players execute run blocks—not pass blocks.

Both plays provide opportunities for as many as an eight-man protection. The plays in the two illustrations specifically use five linemen, one wing, and a fullback protector. Everything on the front side is blocked man-to-man. The play side guard is man-to-man on the near defensive lineman. The play side tackle next to him is man-to-man on the defensive end because we don't want the wing taking on the defensive end alone and we want to release the play side wing into a pass pattern if possible.

Everything on the backside of Double Pull Power pass protection is identical to Power Run. The center back blocks the first defender encountered and the backside guard pulls for the play side linebacker. The backside tackle is inside out man-to-man on

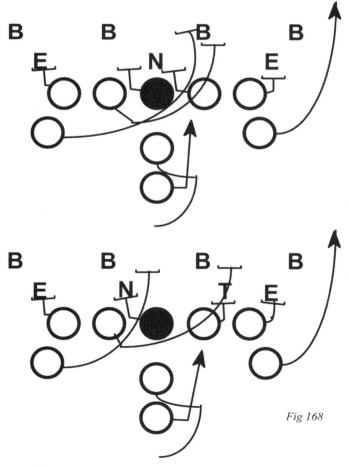

Fig 168

the defensive end and the backside wing pulls for the backside linebacker. These are the same blocks used in Double Pull Power run. Combined they neutralize both inside linebackers.

The quarterback makes the same reverse out as Double Pull Power run. He sets up to pass behind the center after faking to the fullback. The fullback helps clean up on the inside by looking for the play side linebacker first. The play side wing releases into the pattern unless we make a tag for him to stay and protect on level one.

Double Pull Power vs. Blitz

Double Pull Power remains man-to-man on the play side against the blitz. Figure 169 shows the tackle staying with the defensive end inside with the pulling guard taking the edge rusher while the fullback picks up the play side linebacker. The backside wing's primary responsibility is accounting for any backside edge blitzers. He transitions to pulling around and looking for the backside linebacker if there is no backside blitz coming. In total there are three protectors for three gaps covered by the center, tackle, and wing on the backside.

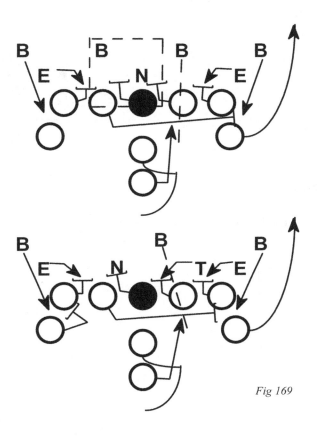

Fig 169

Execution Points of Emphasis

Maximizing the effectiveness of play action passes requires making everything look identical. Pre-snap identification of defensive pressure is important for ensuring effective protection. This read helps the guard decide if he is pulling to the play side linebacker or kicking out the blitzing player off of the edge. Communication also helps the backside wing correctly identify what he is doing.

This protection can become a nine-man protection when the tight end and play side wing are kept in to block. There is also an option for five immediate vertical pass routes if the wing vacates pass protection immediately. Vertical pass routes are explored in greater detail later in the chapter.

SINGLE RECEIVER ISOLATIONS

Go

The most basic and effective route choice for Double Pull Power is a vertical "Go" route on the fake side of the play. We complement this "Go" with a timing route (usually a comeback) on the opposite side. The quarterback read progresses from the Go route to the timing pattern on the backside in the play illustrated (Figure 170).

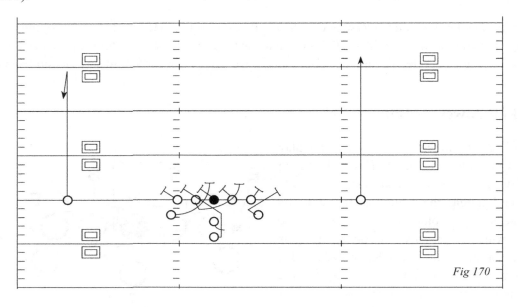

Fig 170

Post

The Post is a second receiver isolation choice. The post route in Figure 171 is highly effective against multiple coverages as well as man-to-man.

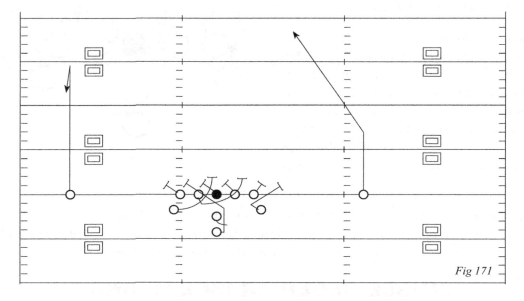

Fig 171

Post-Corner

The third single receiver isolation is a Post-Corner. The Post-Corner becomes more advantageous once the offense sets up the defense with a few standard post routes. The post-corner illustrated (Figure 172) is particularly good against Cover 3 or man-to-man.

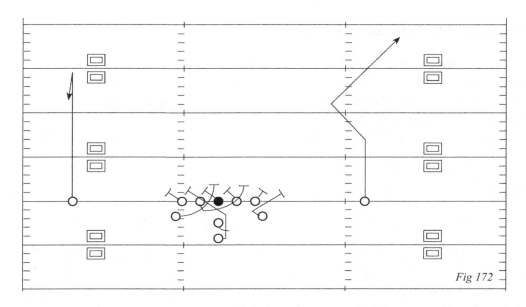

Fig 172

FOUR & FIVE RECEIVER PASS PATTERNS

Inside Seams

Figure 173 shows a four wide receiver combination with inside seams. When executing this play we try to target one of the inside seam routes. The seam we choose is based on the movement of the middle safety. While this combination works best against a single high safety defense it is also a good choice against two high safety coverages because of the timing route to the boundary.

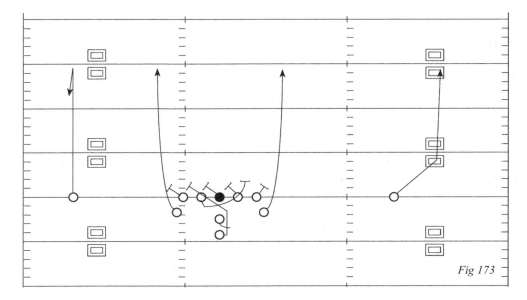

Fig 173

Quarterback Double Pull Power Protection

So far we have examined Double Pull Protection with a fullback exclusively. The Double Pull Power Protection is also available without a fullback (Figure 174). Removing the fullback makes the play a five-man pass protection scheme with a wing staying home as a potential sixth man.

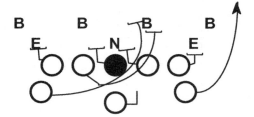

The plays in the following sections feature five immediate pass receivers and vertical pass routes. The backside wing is not wrapping for the backside linebacker in a five-receiver scheme. He instead releases vertically.

Changes to the blocking scheme are not required in this pass protection however. There is man-to-man blocking on the play side and Power blocking on the backside. Running a pure Power Pass Protection package is also an option with the play side down blocking to the backside linebacker and the pulling guard blocking the C-gap on the play side.

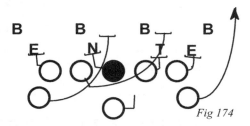

Fig 174

Generally we choose to stay man-to-man on the front side so the pulling guard is able to wrap for the play side linebacker. Against some opponents we find it advantageous for the pulling guard to block off the front side edge. The quarterback follows the same action as the fullback path in a four or five-receiver set. He slide steps to the A-gap and presses downhill toward the line of scrimmage to make sure the play side linebacker triggers on his run fit. The quarterback then delivers the pass after he induces the linebackers to fill.

Five Verticals

Coaches are surprised to learn how much we love Five Verticals. The next illustration (Figure 175) is one of our favorite plays using quarterback Double Pull Power Protection. Notice how the double pull vacates as the backside pull releases to a vertical route. We're relying on the quarterback run action to entice the defense into their run gaps and leaving unhindered access to vertical seams.

Most coaches are familiar with four verticals. Everyone is not familiar with Five Verticals however. We like Five Verticals because it takes advantage of any coverage presented.

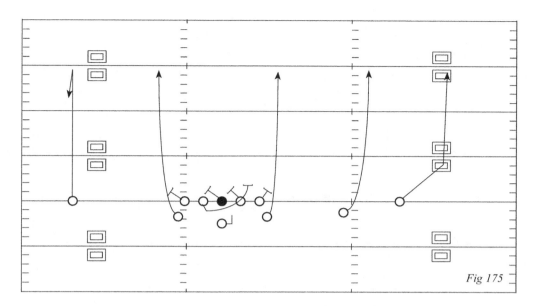

Fig 175

Defenses in Cover 4 assign a linebacker to one of the verticals—typically a wing. This is a difficult job for a linebacker tasked with covering an inside run gap and a wing releasing into a vertical pass route. The result is at least one mismatch against Cover 4 defenses.

We also like Five Verticals against Cover 3 because one of the two verticals down the hash is likely open. Corners are prone to taking the outside verticals away while the free safety accounts for the vertical coming down the middle of the field. It is unlikely in this scenario that the linebackers are able to cover both verticals down the hash marks.

Attacking the middle of the field is still a viable option against Cover 2 (or Tampa 2) by drawing in pass dropping defenders with the run fake.

The same advantage is true across any defensive coverage. Five Verticals (1) create a personnel mismatch for the offense, (2) create open space by spreading the defense, or (3) allow receivers to reach open space by holding the defense with the run fake.

Five Verticals with a Tight End

Figure 176 shows Five Verticals with a Tight End from a personnel grouping of two split ends, two wings, and one Tight End. Five Verticals is not limited to Double Wing formations exclusively. Spread formations work equally well.

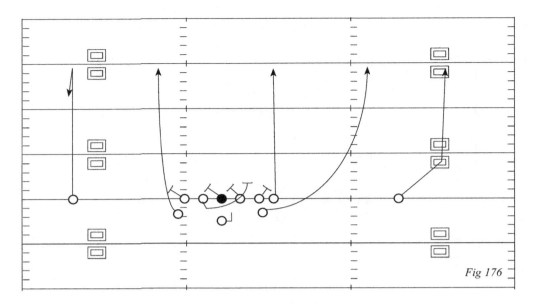

Fig 176

In-Out Route

The "In-Out" Route is a simple play-action pattern. The next illustration (Figure 177) shows the slot receiver releasing inside to sell the block on the outside linebacker. The slot receiver then works outside to the flat once the outside linebacker triggers his run fit. Quarterbacks must get the ball to the slot before anyone else converges on the route. On his read the quarterback throws to the sideline vertical route if the corner comes inside to cover the in-out route. (This read is similar to the one made on Quick Flood.)

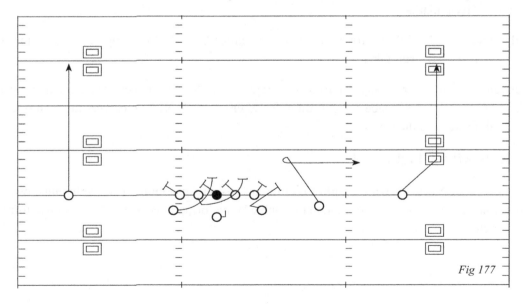

Fig 177

CHAPTER 15: POWER READ PASS

POWER READ PASS: five-man protection
& route combos

Power Read Pass Protection must look identical to Power Read Runs. Power Read Runs are available out of the Flexbone and other Tex-Bone formations—even though they most often come out of a spread look.

The five-man protection on Power Read Run entices defenders to react quickly. Filling linebackers vacate their coverage responsibilities and the open space behind them. This protection naturally spreads the field, sells the run, and provides five immediate receiver options.

POWER READ PROTECTION

Again, Power Read Pass Protection must look identical to Power Read Run. The guard and tackle execute down blocks on the play side. They look for filling linebackers if uncovered at the first level. The pulling guard becomes the C-gap blocker at the point of attack instead of wrapping to the play side linebacker at the second level. This blocking scheme covers the three play side gaps.

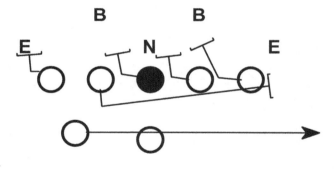

The center and tackle block the A-gap and C-gap on the backside. The B-gap is unaccounted for because of the backside guard pull. Most of the time the backside linebacker scrapes over the top instead of filling the vacated gap however. Is the protection potentially compromised when the backside guard pulls? Yes. The risk is tempered by the big reward of the defense becoming shorthanded if the backside linebacker fills the

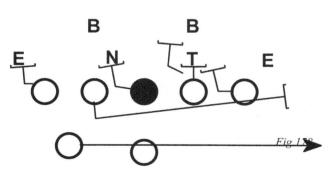

Fig 178

unblocked B-gap though. The two diagrams of Figure 178 demonstrate Power Read Pass Protection.

Power Read Protection vs. Blitz

Power Read Protection covers all gaps against a play side blitz (see Figure 179). The play side tackle must know via a call to stay man-to-man on the defensive end when pressure is applied. This allows the pulling guard to work to the A or C-gap blitzer.

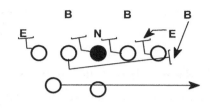

Blitz Answers

Answers are needed when a defense runs a six-man blitz against a five-man pass protection scheme. The following illustration (Figure 180) shows a variety of responses to six-man pressure packages.

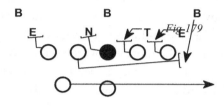

Fig. 179

All protection adjustments must address vulnerabilities on the backside. In our normal Power Read Protection there are only two blockers to the backside. The running back becomes the third blocker when an extra pass rusher joins the play.

The first option (shown in the left column of Figure 180) is for the quarterback is cancel the Power Read sweep action and maintain the rest of the Power Read protection. This blitz answer still influences linebackers by keeping the quarterback run fake in place. The second option (shown in the middle column of Figure 180) is to change the type of fake between the quarterback and running back from a Power Read fake to a dive fake. This allows the running back to pick up the open backside gap once he clears the dive fake. Both of these choices provide six protectors to protect six gaps while maintaining play action run capabilities.

The third protection option (shown in the right column of Figure 180) is to use a traditional Pass Protection of half man on the backside and half zone on the play side. The running back works opposite the offensive tackle on the backside to complete the scheme. This is a great blitz answer if the quarterback knows he's facing cover zero and doesn't need to show play-action influence. (Against covers zero there is no need to sell play-action because defenders aren't in a run fit/zone drop conflict.)

It is advantageous to stick with a Power blocking scheme against any variety of zone blitz. This allows you to sell play-action to defenders responsible for both run gaps and pass zones.

Fig. 180

VERTICAL SEAMS

The primarily route pattern we pair Power Read Protection with is Vertical Seams. We match our Vertical Seams to the coverage we are facing. The next few illustrations show how Vertical Seams are tailored to any coverage.

Figure 181 shows Vertical Seams against a Cover 3 defense. Coaches that use four verticals know that Cover 3 is the defense they would most like to face when running Vertical Seams. Our quarterbacks know to read the middle safety in Cover 3. When the middle safety shades one direction or the other they attempt to target the most uncovered seam. We build a check down built into either side of the field if either of the vertical seams isn't appealing. The check down is a running back stretch to the flat or wide side and the 14-yard comeback to the boundary.

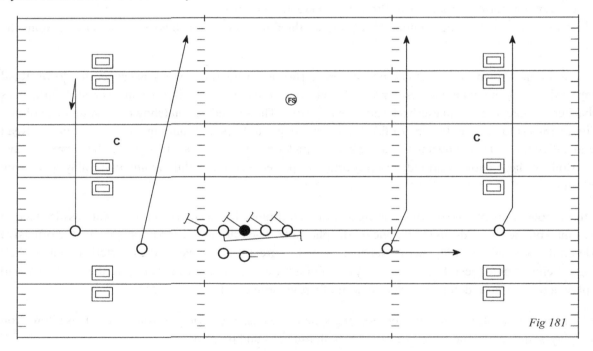

Fig 181

We modify our vertical seams to man coverage rules against Cover 4 (Figure 182). The inside receiver adjusts by widening outside to wrap around above the inside linebacker and in front of the safety. This route is different than what we use to attack Cover 3 defenses.

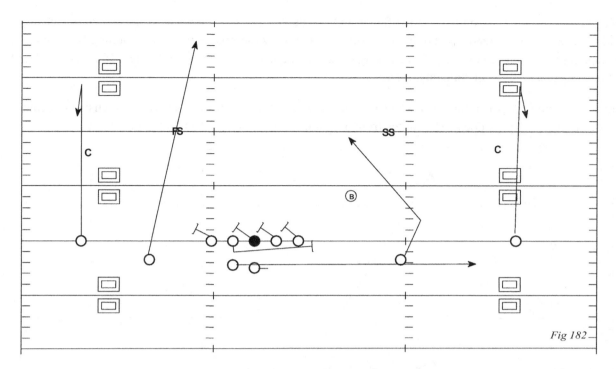

Fig 182

Our quarterback picks one half-field safety in Cover 2 to double team in coverage. The inside seam route in Figure 183 works inside the hash because there is an entire half of the field to work with. The goal is to give the Cover 2 safety too much field to cover at one time. We target the outside vertical if the safety stays tight to the hash. If the safety widens and gets out by the numbers, we target the inside seam.

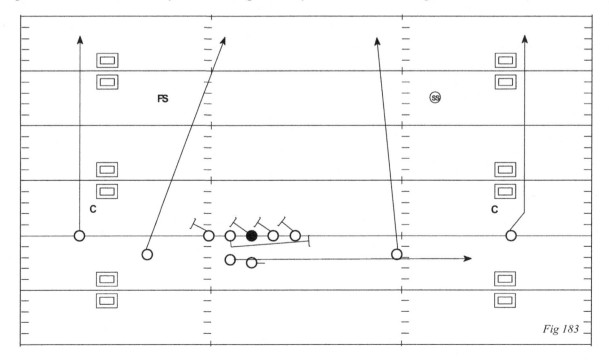

Fig 183

We like to keep the running back in the flat as a check down. Naturally there are times when this changes and the running back needs to stay in and protect. Ultimately the goal is to get the running back into the pass pattern as often as possible. Our running back is always able to release to the flat off the Power Read fake against basic three or four-man rushes.

Figure 184 shows Vertical Seams in a 3x1 formation. A 3x1 formation targets various defensive coverages as well as any 2x2 look does. The routes from 3x1 adjust to coverage just as they do from 2x2.

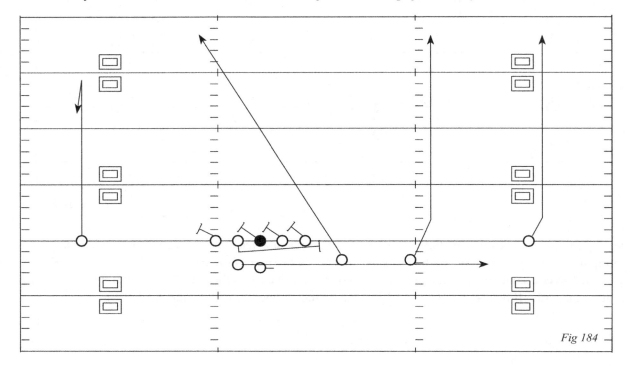

Fig 184

JET MOTION VERTICAL SEASMS

We also like to run Vertical Seams off of Jet Motion (as shown in Figure 185). Vertical Seams with Jet Motion uses the running back to run a seam toward the motion. The slot receiver then works across the field to the backside seam.

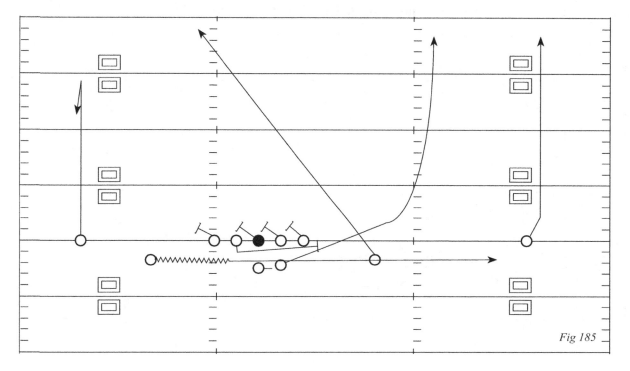

Fig 185

VERTICAL STOPS

T he complement to Vertical Seams is Vertical Stops. Vertical Stops are run to 12 yards before turning and settling. This depth takes advantage of deep coverage trying to stay on top of the Vertical Seams. Figure 186 shows how intermediate zones open up when linebackers are forced to react to the Power Read influence. The quarterback will look inside-out to the side of the running back's route.

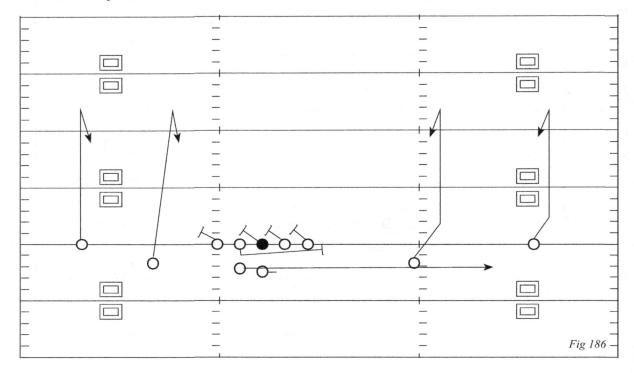

Fig 186

CHAPTER 16: ISO PASSES

ISO PASSES: quick game & drop back pass combos

Iso pass protection must also look identical to Iso runs. Iso pass is a six-man protection regardless of the formation or personnel grouping a team uses. Iso pass protection is **THE** ultimate answer to defensive pressure because it accounts for all six inside gaps through a half man-to-man, half zone scheme.

QB ISO PROTECTION

Figure 187 shows three examples of QB Iso Protection. The play side is man-to-man (common across all Iso protections). The play side guard blocks the near defensive tackle and the offensive tackle is man-to-man on the defensive end. On the backside, the center, guard, and tackle block the A, B and C-gaps. The running back completes the protection by blocking the open gap to the play side. Versus a 3-technique to the play side the running back is responsible for the A-gap and against a 1-technique he takes the B-gap. Against an odd front this block is typically also the B-gap.

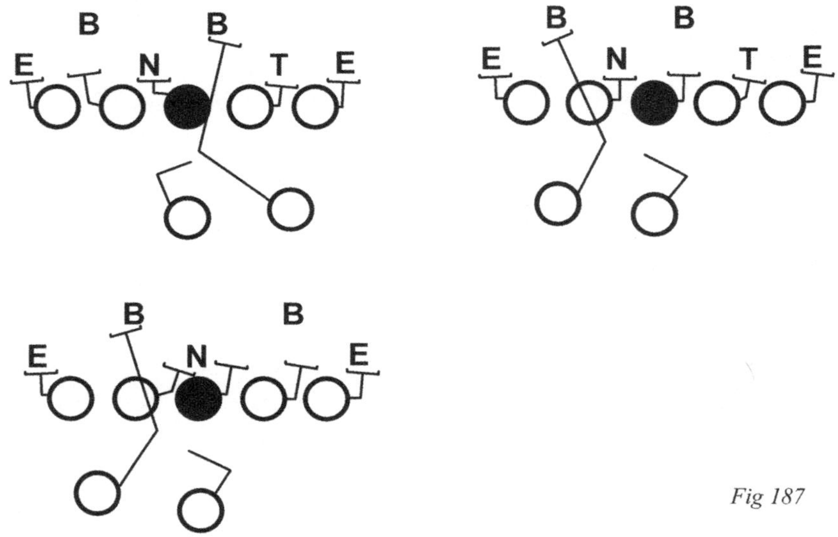

Fig 187

The quarterback fakes an Iso run at the snap by working downhill for two steps towards the backside A-gap. After that he takes two steps back to the middle of the pocket before setting up to throw.

QB Iso Protection vs. Blitz

QB Iso protection is sound against defensive pressure. The backside maintains three players for three gaps while the guard and tackle stay man-to-man on the play side. The offensive guard and tackle stay with the defensive end and defensive tackle that are slanting inside. Their responsibility is to follow the defensive end and defensive tackle no matter where they go on the play (passing off defensive line twists are also an option). The running back picks up the linebacker in whatever gap he shows in. Figure 188 shows the linebacker coming off the edge.

Remember, Iso Pass protection is a half man and half zone with three blockers on both sides of the protection that account for all six inside gaps. We keep Iso protection with run influence against pressure unless the quarterback calls it off and changes to a straight pass protection. If the quarterback does not

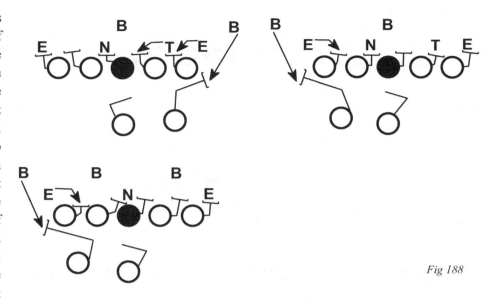

Fig 188

check to a pass protection the offensive linemen still execute their blocks with run demeanor.

We stick with Iso run action against all defenses except Cover 0. Zone dropping players are susceptible to play-action influence. The advantage comes when they vacate space by filling their run gaps.

DIVE ISO PROTECTION

Dive Iso Protection is nearly identical to QB Iso Protection. The difference in backfield action is the running back becomes the Dive Iso instead of the quarterback. Dive Iso action (like quarterback Iso action) is designed to entice linebackers into filling without a change in the blocking scheme. The next illustration (Figure 189) shows the back working off the dive path to block the play side linebacker working through the open gap. The open gap sometimes changes if the defensive line moves.

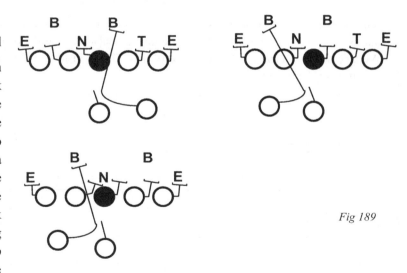

Fig 189

The running back must then adjust to find the linebacker after completing the dive action.

Dive Iso Protection vs. Blitz

The running back works to find a linebacker if the quarterback keeps the dive fake after the mesh occurs. This still leaves three players for three gaps on the backside and three players for three gaps on the play side. Figure 190 shows the straight gap protection scheme on the backside and the man-to-man scheme on the play side.

As previously mentioned, the quarterback is able to call off the run action at any time and check into a straight pass protection. Doing so sends the running back directly where he's needed to pass protect without executing any sort of run fake.

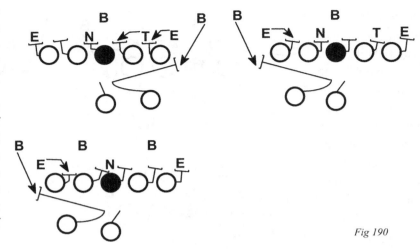

Fig 190

QUICK GAME COMBOS: paired with Quarterback or Dive Iso Protection

We often pair Dive Iso with QB Iso or Power Protection schemes. Changing to Power Protection gives you a different menu of backfield actions to choose from.

Stick

Stick is a staple of the West Coast offense. Figure 191 shows how we slightly modify the outside routes to our preference. The run action holds the inside linebacker and the quarterback reads the outside backer. We take the inside route if it is open every time. If the inside route is not open the quarterback will read the corner as he would on Quick Flood.

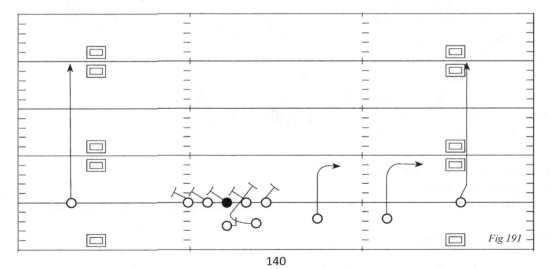

Fig 191

Inside High-Low

The Inside High-Low pattern is a great complement to the Stick play. The middle receiver in Figure 192 wraps inside over the top of the outside linebacker to create a high-low stretch. (This is different than the two out routes in Stick.) If the outside linebacker sits on the inside route we throw the ball into the curl zone behind him. If the outside linebacker drops into the curl zone we throw the Stick route underneath him.

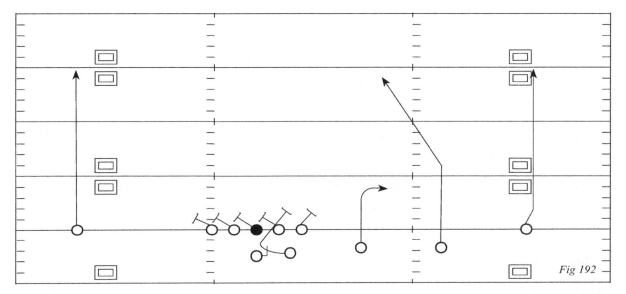

Fig 192

Outside High-Low

The stretch created by the Inside High-Low and Outside High-Low is virtually the same—in this case a high-low on the curl to flat defender (see Figure 193). This high-low stretch is created by a quick dig from the outside receiver and a route working vertically through the curl zone by the middle receiver.

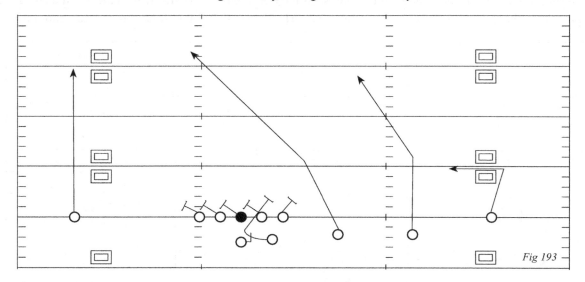

Fig 193

Bubble Screen

The Bubble Screen is one of our favorite plays. It is fast developing, high-speed tempo makes it extremely advantageous. We like to use the Bubble Screen any time there are three-on-three perimeter matchups. Figure 194 shows Bubble Screen out of a 3x1 Open formation to the wide side of the field. We sometimes run this play out of a 2x2 formation as well.

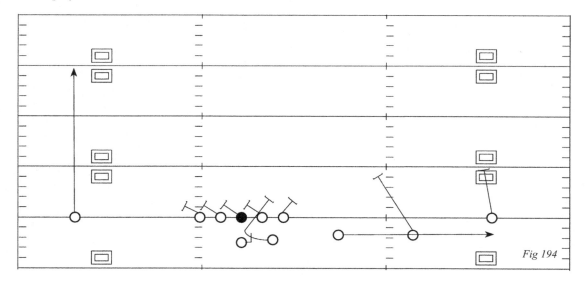

Fig 194

Bubble Vertical

The Bubble Vertical is frequently used as a complement to the Bubble Screen. When the corner or outside linebacker gets aggressive at the line of scrimmage to take away the bubble it leaves a vertical void in the vacated area as shown in Figure 195. There are times that hard charging outside linebackers or corners are difficult to block in the bubble game. In these situations the defense is primed for the Bubble Vertical attack.

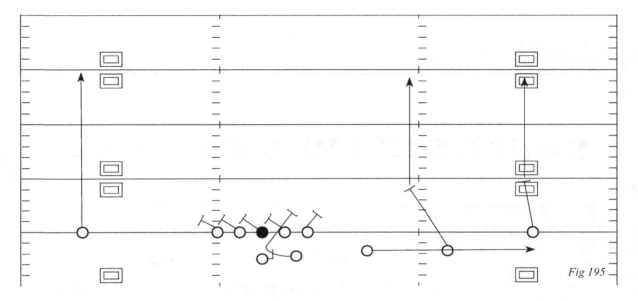

Fig 195

SECTION FOUR

COACHING THE TEX-BONE

17. **Wing & Perimeter Blocking**
18. **Offensive Line Blocking**
19. **Running Back, Quarterback & Receiver Drills**
20. **Practice Organization**
21. **Game Plan Considerations & Ready List**
22. **Game Day Coaching Roles & Charts**

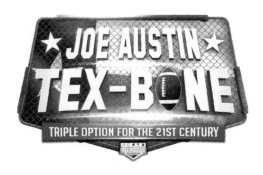

CHAPTER 17: WING & PERIMETER BLOCKING

INDIVIDUAL TECHNIQUES & BLOCKING COMBOS

This chapter explains the blocking techniques and rules we follow before presenting an overview of combination blocking concepts.

BLOCKING PHILOSOPHY

The first blocking rule players learn is "get the ball behind you." This is similar to the basketball concept of staying between your man and the basket. Staying between the defender and the ball puts offensive players in an advantageous blocking position.

Our aiming point on the second and third levels of the defense is always inside-out to the outside number. By staying inside-out our linemen take a position of not allowing a defender to cross the blocker's face in pursuit of the football. In working to the outside number we remain able to reach block at the point of attack. Through practice our players learn to react to forced kick-out situations.

The second blocking rule players learn is "do not let the defender cross your face." With inexperienced players this happens frequently because they stop their feet at the point of attack. Make sure newer players learn to accelerate through contact in order to avoid this critical mistake. We want our players to be proactive—not reactive in blocking situations. We want to establish angles that do the work for us. Our players learn to trust their angles and accelerate at the point of attack by working inside-out to the outside number with the ball behind them.

We do not teach mirror-dodge blocking. We also do not use the term "stalk blocking." We talk about blocking with "no breaks just the gas pedals". The closer we get to the point of contact the faster we move. A mirror block (commonly known as a stalk block) is a reactive block. Our goal is to get the ball behind us, establish an angle that the defender cannot get to the ball without going through us, and then accelerate through contact to the outside number.

Lastly, we want to strike the defender with our thumbs up at the point of attack. This punch provides the best opportunity for sticking the block to the breastplate of the opponent.

2-MAN OPTION BLOCKING RULES

Base Blocking Rule

We establish that the pitch key is, by default, the outside linebacker on the play side of the formation. As a rule we must block any safety on the play side of the formation. The play slot or wing blocks the play side safety in the diagrams of Figure 196 because leaving him free threatens the play.

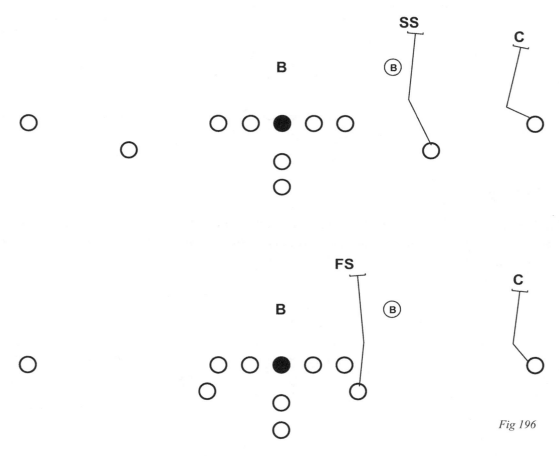

Fig 196

Versus two high safety defenses the play side wing or slot goes directly to the play side safety.

Single high safety defenses put an additional linebacker in the box. Scraping linebackers that leave the box to chase down the pitch phase become a blocking priority for the wing or slot. In Figure 197 we must check for a scraping linebacker before working to the single safety. The wing or slot takes longer to reach the third level when facing a single safety. This gives the wing/slot the ability to look for scrapers before working to the safety.

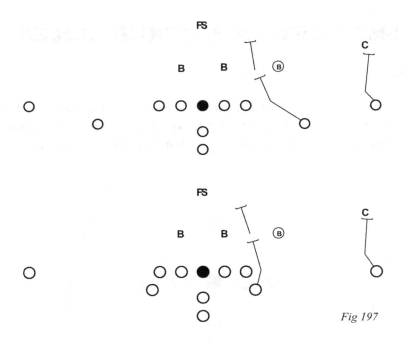

Fig 197

Cross Blocking

Cross blocking is usually an excellent choice because it allows the split end to block any of the defenders usually assigned to a slot or wing. Figure 198 shows cross blocks from a Shotgun Flex-Bone formation and a 2x2 Open formation.

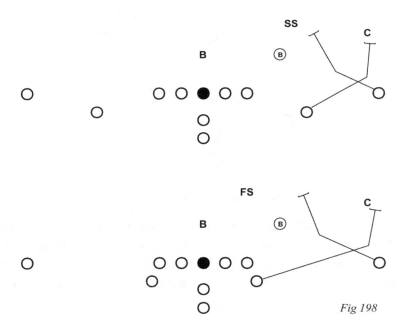

Fig 198

The play side receivers trade responsibilities in both diagrams of Figure 198. The split ends executes a crack block to the safety. Both receivers work flat before gaining ground as they approach the target and accelerate through contact. This block cuts off the defender's outside number and prevents them from getting to the point of attack. The inside player (whether a slot or wing) uses an arc release to reach the corner.

Several defenses (including Cover 0 and Cover 4) put defenders in a situation where they must chase these cross blocks. When the split end leverages inside the corner squeezes down with him. This squeeze makes the arc release and reach block easier for the inside receiver to execute.

The next illustration (Figure 199) shows cross blocking with three receivers. Choosing a two or three-man cross-blocking scheme is predicated on the defense. The split ends leverages inside to crack block the safety and the middle receiver arc releases to the corners. It is important to remember that some defenses make these blocks easier by squeezing the corner down to match the crack block path of the split end.

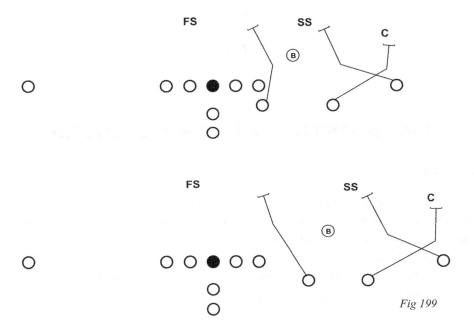

Fig 199

The inside player follows the normal rule of working to the backside safety regardless of whether he is a wing or slot receiver. There is no need for the third blocker to work to the front side safety because the split end already accounts him for. Option teams create three receiver blocking surfaces by using unbalanced formations or by running speed option.

Making the Corner the Pitch Key

There are times when it's advantageous to block the outside linebacker and make the corner the pitch key. Making this change requires a call telling the split end to work down to the safety and the inside receiver to block the outside backer (the typical pitch key). These two instructions (we make the call a single word) now designate the corner as the pitch key (see Figure 200).

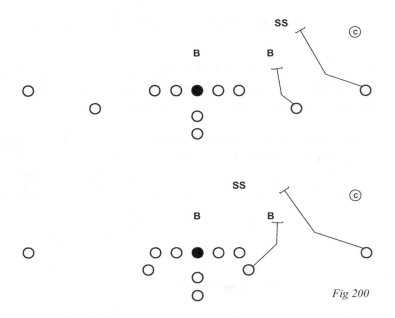

Fig 200

3-MAN OPTION BLOCKING RULES

Base Blocking Rule

Figure 201 shows option blocking with a three-man surface to the perimeter. In both cases, the outside linebacker is the pitch key. All players follow their one or two high safety rules when base blocking. The inside wing checks for a scraping linebacker before working to the single backside safety. With three blockers on the play side the next threat on the backside is most likely the corner chasing the play. Making the outside linebacker the pitchman tells the number two receiver to work straight to the single safety. The split end is then man-to-man on the play side corner.

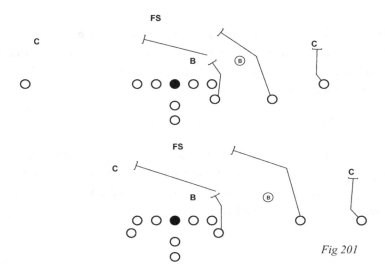

Fig 201

Figure 202 shows the same base blocking scheme against a two high safety defense. We declare the outside linebacker as the pitch key against both single high and two safety high defenses. In both cases the split end is man-to-man on the corner and the slot receiver still works to the nearest safety. The third blocker follows his two high safety rule—whether the player is a wing or a slot. Against two high safeties he works directly to the safety. Notice how the wing/slot in the illustration below works to the backside safety because the second receiver already accounts for the field side safety.

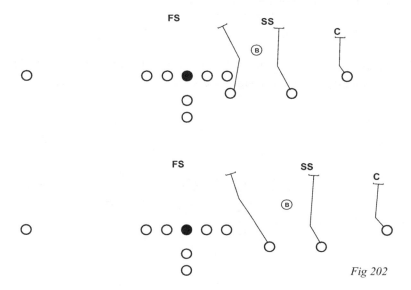

Fig 202

3-MAN SPREAD BLOCKING RULES

Figure 203 show spread blocking rules. There are no players left to option in each illustration. Because of this situation we plan to block all three play side perimeter defenders.

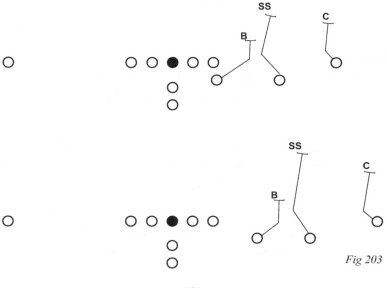

Fig 203

The diagrams in Figure 203 show the split ends working inside first. The diagrams frame the importance of the split end working inside to get the ball behind him. The split end is in an inadequate position to block the corner if the ball isn't behind him. The same is true for the middle receiver. He must work to get the ball behind him prior to working towards the assigned safety.

The ball is already behind the inside slot or wing player by the formational alignment. This is why he begins with an arc block to the assigned outside linebacker.

Cross Blocking

Cross blocking in the spread running game and the option running game are similar. The next illustration (Figure 204) shows cross blocking with two inside receivers.

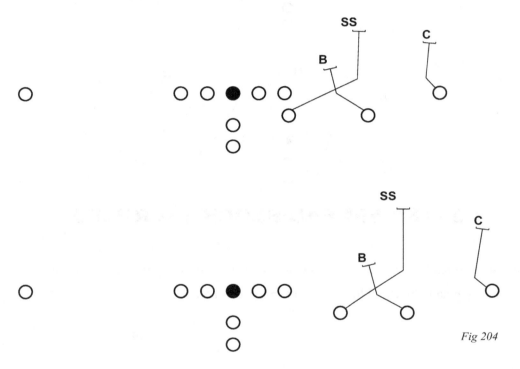

Fig 204

Figure 205 shows a three-man cross blocking scheme. The two outside receivers execute crack blocks on the safety and outside linebacker. The inside receiver then works to the corner. The path of the inside receiver looks odd because he first checks to make sure the outside linebacker and safety are secure before working to the corner.

An added benefit to this path is that the block on the corner is well timed with the play. If the inside receiver works directly to the corner he most likely gets there before the ball does. Blocks become more difficult the longer a player must sustain it. This is true for players inside the box and on the perimeter.

The inside receiver should get to the corner just as the ball is reaching the outside by first securing the linebacker and then the safety. We always want our blocks to engage the defender right as the ball is getting there—not beforehand. This securing makes sure the block is well timed.

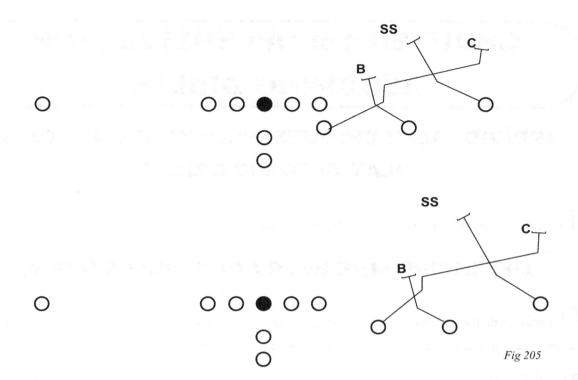

Fig 205

CHAPTER 18: OFFENSIVE LINE BLOCKING DRILLS

INDIVIDUAL TECHIQUES, BLOCKING COMBOS & PLAY SPECIFIC DRILLS

This chapter details how we train our offensive linemen in practice.

OFFENSIVE LINE EVERY DAY DRILLS (EDDs)

Our players do these drills every day—as the name implies. There are very few exceptions to this rule. We run these drills every day regardless of the type of practice (padded or unpadded).

Barrel EDDs

Common 50-gallon trash barrels picked up at any home improvement store are the primary equipment we use to execute our everyday drills. Our EDD barrel drills require seven 50-gallon trash barrels turned upside down and spread out over ten yards. The trash barrels are marked as dashed circles in the following illustrations (starting with Figure 206).

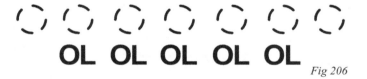

Fig 206

First Step Drill (Figure 207)

In the First Step drill players take one step, reset, and repeat four times with a barrel directly across from them. On the fourth step they release at a 45-degree angle.

The critical skill is learning to gain ground with the first step. Coaching point: teach players to push off of their back foot instead of just reaching out with their front foot. By pushing off the back foot you create more speed and power in departure off the line of scrimmage.

Fig 207

One-Barrel Reach Block (Figure 208)

Players reach block around to the adjacent barrel in the One-Barrel Reach Block drill. Coaching point: it is critical that players gain ground with the first step. Giving linemen a wide aiming point for the reach block (the next barrel over) helps train the reach. After clearing the adjacent barrel they square their shoulders and work towards the goal line at a 45-degree angle.

Fig 208

Two-Barrel Reach Drill (Figure 209)

The two-barrel Reach Drill emphasizes the need to move efficiently while moving laterally. Our goal is for players to take their first step lateral or slightly backwards when reaching. This is not a bucket step however. Bucket steps rarely gain much ground (if any) toward the point of attack. We do not teach our players to step backward. We do recognize that it is sometimes necessary to step backwards when reaching over a long distance however.

Fig 209

Backside Pull Drill (Figure 210)

After realigning the barrels we move to a series of pulling drills. The first drill is our backside pull drill. The drill practices the skip pull by the backside guard on Power. Two players go simultaneously. They skip pull around the adjacent barrel and proceed at a 45-degree angle past the outside number of the level two player represented by the deep barrel.

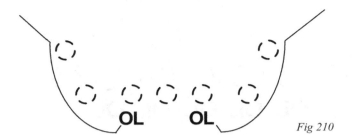

Fig 210

Frontside Pull Drill (Figure 211)

This drill teaches the G Load pull by the play side guard. G Load uses an open step pull instead of a skip pull. After clearing the adjacent barrel the linemen work downfield at a 45-degree angle to the second level.

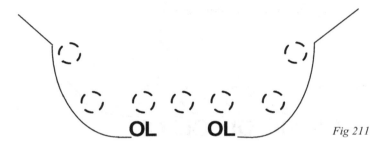

Fig 211

Pull & Trap Drill (Figure 212)

The widest barrels are moved behind the line of scrimmage for the Pull & Trap Drill. This is done to emphasize the drastic angle a pulling guard sometimes takes to kick out a fast penetrating defensive end. The drill trains the player how to adapt to a deep penetrating defender. Our linemen execute a skip pull or open pull in this drill.

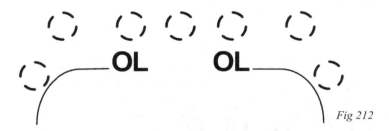

Fig 212

Base Block Drill (Figure 213)

Our EDDs continue without barrels at this point. Two players line-up across from each other for the Base Block drill—one is the offensive player and the other the defensive player. The offensive player steps, engages, and steers the defender on command. We steer by taking the defender wherever he wants to go. Coaching point: to avoid holding penalties we do not use a push-pull steer. Instead we turn our hands like a steering wheel. One hand pulls down and one hand pushes up.

Fig 213

Steering is an important part of opening holes. We achieve the steer without offensive linemen putting their rear in the hole. This is done to avoid giving the defender a two-way release by turning their shoulders. It also makes the hole smaller in terms of space to run the ball through.

Effective steering is the best way to create space. Several players are able to work the Base Block Drill at the same time in pairs. Coaching point: the Base Block Drill works best when linemen step in both directions.

Guard & Tackle Iso Pull Drill (Figure 214)

The last EDD (Every Day Drill) is our Iso pull. Guards pull to Iso block on Power and tackles pull to Iso block on Tackle Pull Iso. The play side guard blocks the near defensive tackle in this drill. If the guard works to the A-gap, the pulling player works through the B-gap. If the guard works to the B-gap, the puller works through the A-gap. The puller must gather information as he moves to where he fits into the line of scrimmage. Coaching point: pullers need to stay square to the line of scrimmage.

We practice both guard and tackle pulls. Though not every day, we will also practice center pulls. We also practice pulls to the A-gap and B-gap as well as pulls to the right and left.

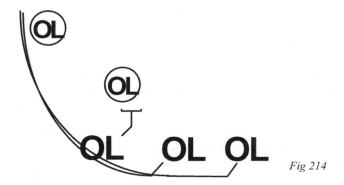

Fig 214

PLAY SPECIFIC DRILLS

G-T Counter Drill (Figure 215)

We work a drill that uses both backside pullers and the play side tackle to train G-T Counter. The backside tackle's inside release gives the pullers a visual cue as to how much space they get to operate. The pullers then work to block the defensive end and the play side linebacker.

The pulling guard must recognize if the defensive end is squeezing and log him. The tackle must also recognize the log and pull around to reach the second level linebacker. If the defensive end works up field, the pulling guard kicks out while the tackle works underneath. Coaching point: the tackle must learn to get more depth than the guard to get the time and space needed to react to the guard's block.

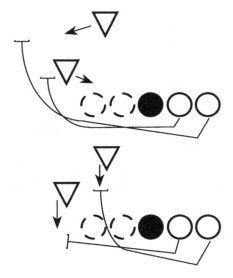

Fig 215

Combo Block Drill (Figure 216)

We use the combination block most often on the Double Pull Power. To teach the combo block we set up a two-on-one drill with two offensive players working against one defender. The offensive players begin by both stepping toward the defensive player. The goal is for the two blockers to get rear-to-rear so the defender cannot split them. Their intent is to get vertical movement toward the end zone. The inside blocker stays with the single defender when he slants to the inside. The outside player then comes off of the double team block and works to level two.

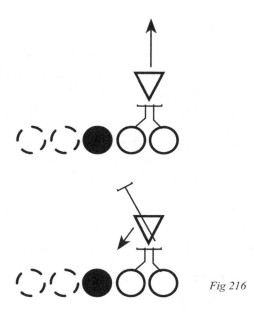

Fig 216

G Load Drill (Figure 217)

To teach the play side fold block on G Load we built a drill that utilizes the play side guard, tackle, and the fullback. The goal is to block the defensive end and the play side linebacker.

The drill starts by the tackle releasing inside and the guard pulling around him for the defensive end. The guard logs the defensive end if he squeezes. The fullback then works outside of the log and underneath the kick out to the play side linebacker on the second level. Coaching point: in game situations the second level block by the fullback is likely a cut.

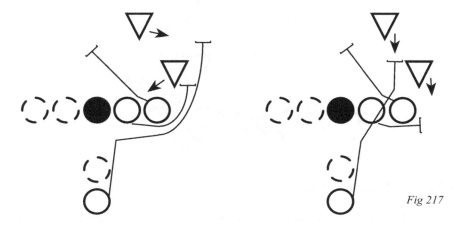

Fig 217

Veer Drill (Figure 218 and 219)

The Veer drill trains the play side guard and tackle to handle the defensive tackle and the play side linebacker. The set-up includes the play side guard and tackle working against three defenders (the defensive tackle, defensive end, and play side linebacker). The drill starts with the guard blocking the near defensive tackle and the offensive tackle releasing inside to the play side linebacker.

This drill trains linemen to combat two different defensive scenarios. Scenario one: the linebacker stays home in the B-gap when the defensive end works up field to contain. This scenario is easier for the tackle to handle by working to the outside number of the linebacker.

The more difficult scenario two is the squeeze-scrape, or gap exchange defense. When this happens, the defensive end squeezes down to take the B-gap and the linebacker scrapes outside to play the C-gap. To combat this scenario the tackle must take a banana release to the scraping linebacker.

Fig 218

The Veer Option chapter explained how the blocking scheme changes if the defensive tackle is a B-gap player (3-technique). We prepare for this change by practicing the fold block against a 3-technique. The tackle down blocks the defensive tackle and the guard pulls to the play side linebacker in this situation.

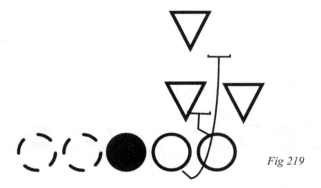

Fig 219

Double Pull Power Drill (Figure 220)

This combines the Combo and the Skip Pull Power blocks into one drill. The guard and tackle execute a double team on the play side 3-technique defensive tackle. Coaching point: we use a barrel as a placeholder for the center. Putting a player in that spot to practice back blocking is also an option.

The pulling guard must read the movement of the double team to know where he inserts into the line of scrimmage to attack the play side linebacker. The guard then takes the first opening he sees. He pulls tight if the double team moves vertically. The guard potentially pulls slightly wider if the double team moves laterally however.

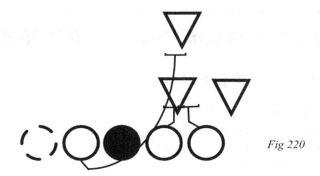

Fig 220

Coaching point: previous sections showed drills practicing these skills separately. In a time crunch this drill is effective at training both the combo and skip pull blocks at the same time.

Pass Protection Drill (Figure 221)

Our final drill is Drop Back Pass Protection. We teach this by working against one-on-one pass rushes by our defensive linemen. Coaching point: the offensive player works to keep his shoulders as square as possible while punching with the thumbs up.

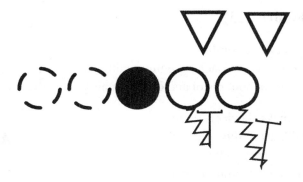

Fig 221

CHAPTER 19: RUNNING BACK, QUARTERBACK, RECEIVER DRILLS

TRIPLE OPTION DRILL PROGRESSION

Introducing the Dive Phase (Figure 222)

Splitting the triple option into smaller component parts is important when first installing the Tex-Bone offense. The first element to teach is quarterback and fullback coordination.   We begin this chapter with teaching the dive path without any reads. This allows the quarterback and the fullback to learn how to step without any external distractions.

The dashed line players in the illustrations are excluded from the drill and all the solid line players are included in the drill.   We like to use a commercially bought offensive line spacers for our placeholders.

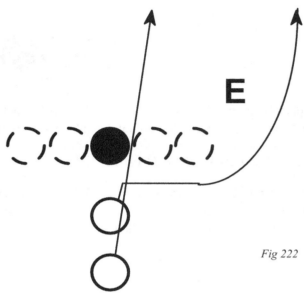

Fig 222

Adding the Dive Key (Figure 223)

Once the quarterback and fullback are comfortable with the mesh we add in the dive key. Coaching point: additional parts of the play are not added at this time. We practice the dive key from both pistol and offset running back alignments.

The quarterback is learning to make the decision to keep the ball or give to the fullback at this stage of progression.   Coaching point: remember, the fullback gets the football unless he is going to get tackled by the dive key.

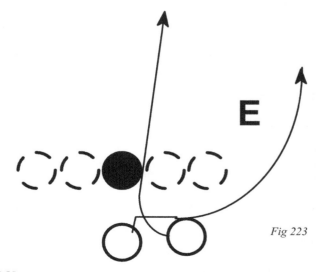

Fig 223

Introducing the Pitch Key (Figure 224)

The pitch key is introduced once the dive phase is performed well by the quarterback and the fullback. This drill does not use a pitch back—the quarterback runs through the alley each time because the pitch key is told to always cover the pitch. Coaching point: this phase of learning is an important piece of quarterback development. We are teaching the quarterback to attack the alley after he pulls the ball from the dive. The quarterback must understand that in the pitch phase the ball is his unless threatened by the pitch key.

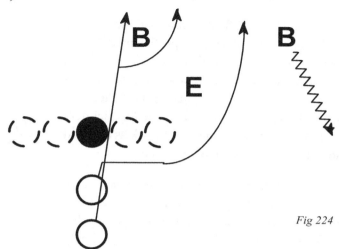

Fig 224

The fullback learns to cut off of the block after he receives the ball on the dive. Coaching note: instruct the dive key to mix up the read keys. He cannot always give a pull key to the quarterback. The quarterback must learn to transition his eyes from the dive key to the pitch key. Adding a secondary read for the fullback is also an option. This secondary read is the block on the play side linebacker.

Introducing the Pitch Back - The Full Triple Option Drill (Figure 225)

Introducing the pitch back is the next step after the quarterback understands how to read the dive key and gets his eyes on the pitch key. Adding the pitch back allows you to run a full triple option play with both a dive phase and the pitch phase.

The illustration shows the pitch player as a wing a on the backside of the play. Coaching point: there are many more options in terms of pitch player alignment for the Pitch Back drill. (These looks are discussed later in the chapter.)

The drill begins with the fullback and quarterback dive mesh. The quarterback reads the dive key for a give or pull read. The fullback then reads his secondary key in terms of cutting off the play side linebacker at the second level. The quarterback attacks the alley if he keeps the ball after the dive phase.

Coaching point: in this drill the pitch key either widens to take the pitch back or runs to the alley and forces the quarterback to make the pitch.

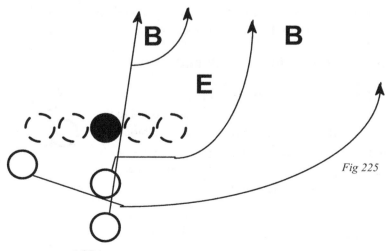

Fig 225

Introducing Backfield Actions & Motions (Figure 226)

Adding various backfield actions and motions are possible once your players are proficient at the full triple option drill detailed previously. The preseason is a great opportunity to put in some of the actions you anticipate running throughout the season. This gives you practice time for backfield actions and motions during game week as opposed to losing time teaching individual skills.

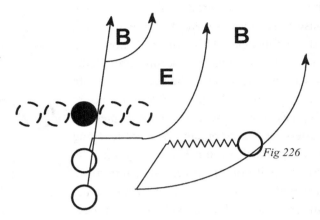

Fig 226

Coaching point: the coaches or players that serve as the dive key and pitch key in all of our triple option drills receive explicit instructions as to what they do. Allowing dive and pitch keys to randomly develop is also an option. Coaches are best served to instruct players to execute specific keys when practicing for a specific opponent overall.

Fullback Load Drill (Figure 227 and 228)

The next practice progression is to run the Full Triple Option drill with a fullback load. Our fullback load assigns the fullback to block the dive key. We enter the pitch phase of triple option once this happens.

The quarterback takes the ball around the edge into the pitch phase if the fullback is able to log or cut block the dive key. If the fullback is forced to kick out, the quarterback reacts and comes underneath the dive key to the second level. Coaching point: the quarterback coming underneath does not mean the pitch phase is eliminated. Quarterbacks must learn to keep sight of the pitch even after the play is forced up field and underneath the kick out block.

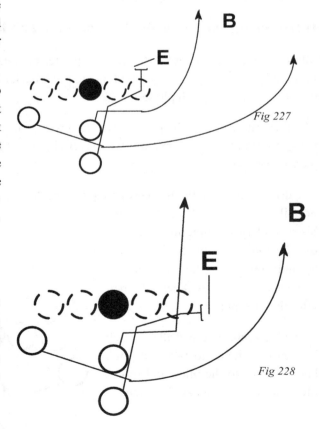

Fig 227

Fig 228

Fullback Lead (Figure 229 and 230)

In fullback lead we assign the fullback to block the play side linebacker. The fullback pulls around to the linebacker if the pulling guard is able to log block the defensive end. When the pulling guard is forced to kick out, the fullback reacts and comes underneath to reach the play side linebacker.

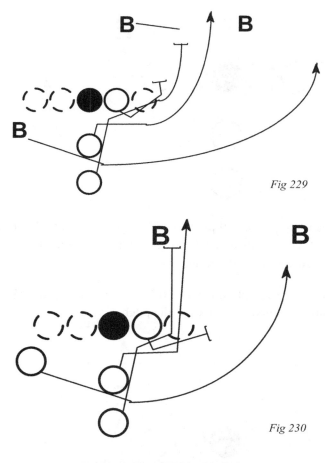

Fig 229

Fig 230

SPEED OPTION

We utilize a variety of pitch players aligning in a variety of positions in the Speed Option game. In Speed Option the quarterback attacks the outside number of the pitch key—in this case the defensive end.

The quarterback's first job is to get the ball pitched. The running back gains width as fast as possible to work downhill towards the end zone when accepting the ball from the quarterback.   Coaching point: we want the pitch executed on a flat trajectory.

Figure 231 demonstrates Speed Option from an offset alignment. It shows the quarterback keeping the ball after attacking the outside number of the pitch key.

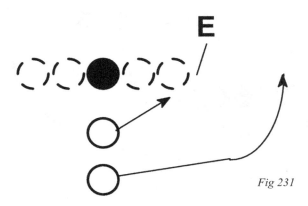

Fig 231

The quarterback is endeavoring to get the ball pitched. The running back will gain width as fast as possible so that he can work downhill towards the end zone while accepting the ball from the quarterback. We want to pitch to be executed very on a flat trajectory.

Figure 232 shows the training of speed option from an offset alignment. It also shows the quarterback keeping the ball after attacking the outside number of the pitch key.

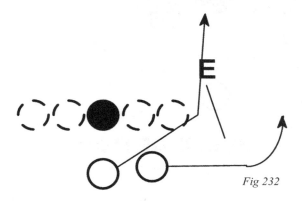

Fig 232

POWER READ DRILL

O ur Power Read drill features a defensive end that serves as the dive key (see Figure 233). Because this is a double option play there is no pitch key. The running back starts by taking his sweep path across the face of the quarterback. The quarterback then gives the ball to the running back if the dive key does not work up field quickly to take the sweep away.

Coaching point: it is the sweep player's ball on Power Read unless the dive key takes the give away. The quarterback pulls the ball and runs the dive path when the dive key gets enough depth and width to take the sweep away.

A quick mesh makes it difficult for the defensive end to take away the sweep. Quick movement makes it difficult for the end to cover the sweep even when it's his assignment on the play.

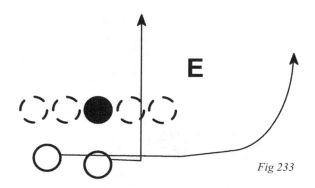

E

Fig 233

JET MOTION DRILL

The Jet Motion drill is nearly identical to the Power Read drill (see Figure 234). We bring a slot receiver in motion to mesh with the quarterback and put a running back in an offset position for the Jet Motion drill. The offset back practices his arc release to the play side outside linebacker. Coaching point: on all versions of Power Read (including Jet Motion) the contain player remains the dive key we read.

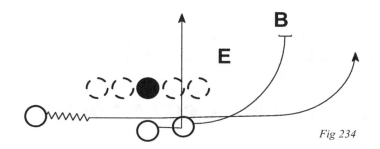

B

E

Fig 234

QUARTERBACK ISO DRILL

The Quarterback Iso drill (Figure 235) features an offset running back and a quarterback working against a play side linebacker. We use this drill to teach the footwork and blocking techniques required to isolate properly.

Coaching point: We don't put a guard in front of the running back when first teaching this drill. If there is a guard in front of the running back he must learn to identify where the guard is blocking. The running back must also learn to identify which gap is open for him to reach the play side linebacker.

We progress to gap identification only after the running back learns how to take a good blocking path.

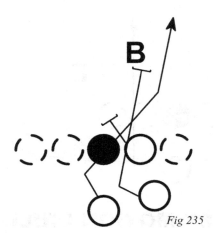

Fig 235

It is extremely important for the lead back to learn how to get the ball behind him. The offset running back works to the inside first to successfully do this. After getting the ball behind him, the back works inside-out to the outside number of the linebacker.

Coaching point: when adding a guard to that drill the running back must learn to read the guard's block. The running back needs work through the A-gap to the play side linebacker if the guard works to the B-gap to block the 3-technique.

Quarterbacks learning Iso know to take two counter steps to the opposite A-gap. Stepping too flat makes him arrive late at the point of attack. The quarterback cannot entice linebackers to shift away from the play if he does not get far enough towards the A-gap.

DOUBLE PULL POWER DRILL

Ball carriers learn how to react to the double team in the Double Pull Power drill (Figure 236). We run this as Quarterback Double Pull Power or Fullback Double Pull Power. The drill starts with a guard and tackle simulating the double team. The ball carrier learns to stay tight to the inside if the double team pushes vertical. If the double team works across his face or horizontally, the ball carrier learns to bounce the ball slightly to the outside.

Coaching point: it is important that the ball carrier gets behind the double team to create options in terms of blocking based on the movement created by the double team.

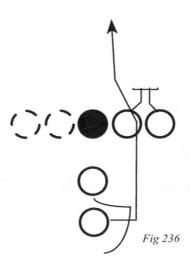

Fig 236

PASS ROUTES WITH READ SIMULATIONS

Any pass play in the Tex-Bone is teachable by setting up a drill that simulates the reads the quarterback makes. In pass route drills with read simulations the quarterback will work with all the wide receivers involved in the read progression. If possible, it's useful to get the running backs with the quarterback so they learn to make play action passes look identical to run plays.

Coaching note: we generally use coaches or other players to simulate the defenders that are read.   In Quick Flood we assign a coach to play the role of the cornerback for example. If the corner sits near line of scrimmage to cover the out route, the quarterback learns to throw the ball to the vertical hole down the sideline between the corner and the safety. To teach this hole-throw we put another coach at the safety position.   When the cornerback drops and runs with the vertical route down the sideline, the quarterback learns to throw the ball quickly to the out route.

POINT OF ATTACK DRILL

The Point of Attack Drill teaches offensive players how to engage a defender. The fundamental coaching points are: (1) strike the defender with the elbows in and thumbs up, (2) keep your head to the outside of the defender as to reach or "hook" the defender, and (3) keep your shoulders square to the line of scrimmage and push the defender toward the goal line.

The drill is set-up by placing a defensive player and an offensive player in close proximity, but offset slightly. As this drill is intended to teach only the engagement portion of blocking it is important that the distance between the players be close.

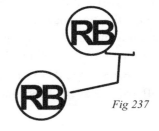

Fig 237

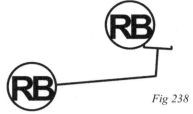

Fig 238

The first version of the drill (Figure 237) will position the offensive player two lateral steps away from the defender. On command, the offensive player will engage the defensive player being certain to accomplish the three goals stated above.

The second version of the drill (Figure 238) will place the offensive player two yards from the defender. On command, the offensive player will work laterally and engage the defender. Again, the blocker must be diligent to accomplish the stated goals.

BLOCKING LEVERAGE DRILL

The Blocking Leverage Drill is an everyday drill for our outside wide receivers. It is also a weekly drill for our inside wide receivers and running backs. The goal of this drill is to train level two and level three blocking angles. The goal of every perimeter blocker is to get the ball behind them right away. Players can correlate this skill to basketball defense where the idea is to stay between their man and the basket. For our purpose, the basket is the football and their man is the defender that they will block. The basket doesn't move, but the football does, and therefore this skill requires a lot of repetitions. If an offensive player is not positioned between the ball and the defensive player he is at a disadvantage because the defender can attack the ball from any direction. Conversely, when an offensive player positions themselves between the ball and the defensive player they are now in an advantageous position because the defender must run around the offensive player to try to get to the football. The offensive player can use his advantageous positioning to funnel the defender where he wants him to go.

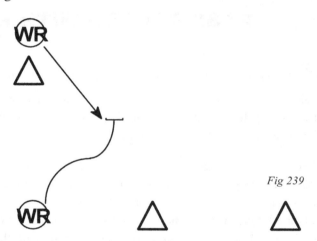

Fig 239

Our philosophy is that we always want to funnel players to the outside, and then beat them to the intersection point where the defender will get to the ball carrier. This drill teaches this skill.

Figure 239 shows the set-up for the blocking leverage drill. Two players will participate; one as the offensive player and one as the defensive player. In the illustrations the offensive player is on the bottom and the defensive player is on the top. At the beginning of the drill the defensive player will run to the nearest cone that is aligned adjacent to the offensive player. This cone signifies the intersection

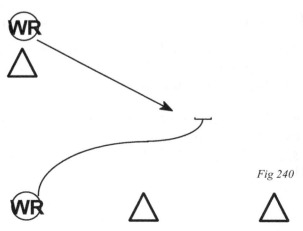

Fig 240

point where the defender would intersect the ball carrier if not impeded.

The offensive players will take an inside-out patch to intercept and block the defender. The inside-out path is significant because this path forces, or funnels, the defender to the outside by cutting of the inside path to the ball. By taking the appropriate inside-out angle the blocker has positioned the ball behind him and forced the defender to his outside. The offensive player will then take the appropriate angle to intercept the defensive player before he gets to the cone.

When the block is joined, the offensive player will strike with his elbows in and thumbs up. Most importantly, he will engage the outside number of the defender so he can "hook" the defender, thus allowing the ball carrier to continue on his path. The worst case scenario is that the offensive player will have to "wash" the defensive player past the intersection point. The ball carrier can adjust his path accordingly.

This drill will then be repeated with the defender aiming for the wider cone (Figure 240) signifying a wide intersection point. The offensive player must now adjust his angle and path accordingly.

TAG DRILL

The Tag Drill is the advanced progression of the Blocking Leverage Drill and appears in Figure 241. In the Tag Drill, the defensive player is free to choose and point of attack any path they choose. The ability of the offensive player to get the ball behind them, force the defender to the outside, then "hook" them at the point of attack is tested.

To be successful at this drill, the offensive blocker must learn to be patient to the point of attack as to not be faked by the defender. Once the offensive player has successfully funneled the defender to the outside, he must accelerate as contact is engaged.

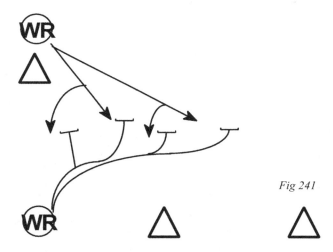

Fig 241

Accelerating at the point of attack gives the offensive player the speed and force necessary to win the physical match-up with the defensive player.

STANCE & START CHASE DRILL

The Stance and Start Chase Drill is a competitive drill that teaches players to move efficiently at the beginning of the play. Inefficient movement, as in taking extra steps of misplaced steps, wastes valuable time and this drill is a great way to teach players to eliminate waste. We use this drill with all perimeter position groups – quarterback, running back and wide receiver.

As Figure 242 shows, two players will line up behind each other with one yard between them. On command (or when the ball moves) the two players will race to a finish line. The finish line can be any distance and we typically set the finish ten yards away. If the player in front takes extra steps or moves inefficiently at the beginning of the chase he will likely be caught by the player chasing him. The opposite is also true. If the chasing player moves inefficiently they will not be able to catch the player in front of them.

Coaches should be looking for all of the following components of the player's release from their starting position: body lean, arm position, ankle and knee bend, width of stance and directional pointing of feet.

This drill is an excellent opportunity to add competition to practice. A reward for winning or a penalty for losing can be added. Making the drill competitive will ensure that players give their best effort in the chase.

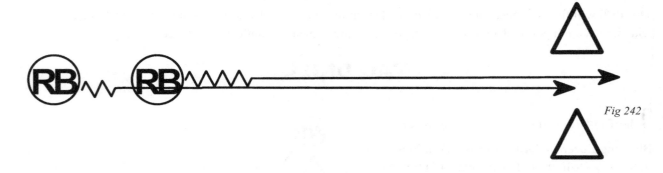

Fig 242

CHAPTER 20: SYSTEM & PRACTICE ORGANIZATION

PRE-SEASON PREPARATION

One of the most important pre-season duties for an offensive coordinator is preparing the training camp installation schedule. Figure 243 shows the training camp installation schedule my team used in 2018. It an eight-day offensive installation schedule. There is nothing significant or symbolic about the choice of an eight-day install. Length often varies based on individual team needs and rules designating the amount of practice time allowed in the pre-season.

The illustration also demonstrates how we set a specific theme for each practice. We taught Power Option on our first day. We partnered it with Power Option Pass Protection from 2x1 or Flexbone formations only. We added in a few simple motions only because most of our players were returners familiar with these concepts.

We like to add details to our install schedule such as when defensive line games are added. This helps us train more effectively against defensive pressure. We also add in the dress specifications for practice (pads, no-pads, helmets, etc.) once other specifics are finalized. Based on the specific plays we are installing the decision is made whether to include any 7-on-7 time or inside run practice time.

Coaching point: play action heavy offenses don't necessarily need a 7-on-7 period specifically devoted to practicing it every day. Training play-action is generally more effective in 11-on-11 situations. Practicing play action passes in 7-on-7 with no run keys is sometimes detrimental to the progression of your quarterbacks. Remember, practice the way you play as often as possible.

Fall 2018 Offensive Install

	1	2	3	4	5	6	7	8
RUN	Power Option	Double Pull Power	Power Read	Iso	G Load	Speed Option	Veer	Counter
PASS	Power Option	Double Pull Power	Power Read	Iso Passes	G Load Passes			
PRO	Power	Double Pull Power	5-Man Power	Dive Iso QB Iso	G Load			
FORMATION	Flexbone 2x1s	Em. Flexbone	3x1s 2x2s	3x2s				
MOTION	Flip Jump		F, Z, H					
DEFENSE		DL Games				Blitz		
DRESS								
7 on 7	No	No	Yes	Yes (short)	No	No	Yes	No
INSIDE	Yes	Yes	Yes	Yes	Yes	Yes	No	No

Fig 243

Creating Installation Schedules

Creating an effective installation schedule requires careful consideration before proceeding. Three factors detailed below are worth studying in particular.

Consideration one: adjusting and extending the installation schedule. The length of the installation schedule is adjustable and extendable to as much as 11-13 days. Separating the run install from the pass install allows for an area of expansion. Instead of installing both Power Option runs and Power Option passes on the first day of practice a team might install Power Option runs on the first day and Power Option passes on the second. The separation then continues throughout the entire installation schedule. Extending your installation schedule to 11-13 days is a good idea when installing a new offensive system. A separate extended schedule is also advisable for new or younger players in an existing offense.

Consideration two: compressing or accelerating the installation schedule. Compressing or accelerating the schedule to as few as five days is also an option for veteran teams. This scenario calls for installing everything Power related in one day—including Power Option runs, Power Option passes, Double Pull Power runs, Double Pull Power passes, and Power Read runs and passes. This compression is also good idea for spring practice with existing personnel.

Consideration three: creating a double installation schedule. Creating a double installation schedule refers to the idea of running the entire installation schedule twice. Setting an appropriate pace is important. The process of working through the entire installation phase twice is meaningful for some teams.

A double installation schedule does not mean running the same plays two days in the row. Double installation means running the entire schedule from start to finish twice. If a team is running a five-day installation schedule the first day and the sixth day of practice are identical. Running a double installation schedule increases overall player comprehension and learning absorption—especially for new players. The process also gives players two opportunities for supporting meetings, film study, walk throughs, and chances to run the plays. Increased exposure to these teaching tools generally leads to better understanding and execution.

Individual Period Plans

The offensive coordinator must also develop a plan for teaching skills during individual practice periods. This plan is ideally made with the input of each position coach respectively. Each position coach lists skills and the amount of time needed to teach the skills. This information goes into the practice plan. Player learning styles is an important consideration when developing individual period plans. Creating a plan that matches the teaching expertise of the coaching staff is also an important factor to consider.

Installation schedules are heavily influenced by the amount of time required to teach position-specific skills. Teams with fewer veterans and large groups of new players need more time to learn position group skills and the offense overall. These scenarios require longer and often more detailed installation schedules. Teams with large numbers of experienced returning players are often able to shorten the installation schedule because the teaching time demands are less. Dividing new players and veteran players during practice to focus on different skills based on various levels of progression and experience is also a possibility.

Figure 244 shows our basic offensive practice plan template. All our coaches put their individual drills in the proper boxes on the plan. In some cases this is as simple as writing "EDD" for everyday drills.   Our offensive line coach (Tom Ross) frequently writes EDD for his individual period plan as our offensive coaches know what his every day drills are.

PIRATE FOOTBALL
Offensive Practice Plan
4:55 PM 6:33 PM

Opponent:	TLU	Practice:	Wednesday	Dress:	Helmet
Meetings:	4:10 PM	End:	4:40 PM		
PERIOD	OL	TE	WR	QB	RB
Warm/Walk 4:55 PM 8					
Indy 5:03 PM 12					
WATER					
Inside 5:15 PM 15					
D 7 on 7 5:30 PM 10					
WATER					
O 7 on 7 5:40 PM 9					
Unit 5:49 PM 28					
Specials 6:17 PM 10					
Stretch 6:27 PM 6					
6:33 PM					

Meeting- 7:00

Announcements: *Fig 244*

The practice plan for each position group allows the entire staff to know what individual skills are taught and for how long. Plans for group work are also made as well. We note on the practice plan if the running backs, fullbacks, and wings are getting together to run triple option drills for example.

The tight end position group is unique because they often split their individual time between the offensive line and wide receivers. This time division is planned out ahead of time and documented on the daily practice plan.

Scripting Training Camp Practices

I always prefer to script as much of training camp as possible in advance. Naturally, there are times when I go back and make adaptations to the original practice script. When I do it's always easier to make revisions to an existing plan than it is to write a new script throughout fall camp.

Training camp is a busy time with tons of activities beyond practice. Finding time to prepare a detailed script alongside these other demands is extremely difficult, albeit impossible—especially for head coaches. Scripting beforehand provides the advantage or making sure all the formations, plays, and situations needed for the upcoming season are included in both the installation practice schedule and the daily practice plan.

What scripting "on-the-fly" seemingly gains in flexibility it loses in consistency and effectiveness. Scripting as you go runs the risk omitting important details critical for offensive success. This is especially true in the pre-season when time is at a premium. Leaving out important details due to a planning error leads to lost time and inefficient/ineffective player development. Predesigned installation schedules with corresponding practice plans provide structure, consistency, and smooth transitions.

Figure 245 shows one of our practice script templates. We use a variety of practice script templates for different points of the season. The template in the illustration contains four scripted periods: (1) inside run, (2) walk through, (3) 7-on-7, and (4) team. We leave some room for other notes or reminders on the bottom. We also leave space for personnel group information or anything else we need to include in the bottom right hand corner of the script.

INSIDE

#	Hash		Personnel & Play	Front	Blitz/Game	Coverage
1	R	D&D				
2	R		Personnel & Play			
3	R	QB				
4	L			Front	Blitz/Game	Coverage
5	L					
6	L					
7	L					
8	R					
9	R					
10	R					
11	L					
12	L					
13	L					
14	L					
15	L					
16	L					
17	L					
18	R					
19	R					
20	R					
21	R					
22	R					
23	R					

Walk Thru

#	Hash				
1	R				
2	R				
3	R				
4	R				
5	L				
6	L				
7	L				
8	L				
9	L				
10	L				
11	R				

7 on 7

#	Hash				
1	L				
2	L				
3	L				
4	L				
5	L				
6	L				
7	L				
8	R				
9	R				
10	R				
11	R				
12	R				
13	R				
14	R				

TEAM

#	Hash				
1	L				
2	L				
3	L				
4	L				
5	L				
6	R				
7	R				
8	R				
9	R				
10	R				
11	L				
12	L				
13	R				
14	R				
15	R				
16	L				
17	L				
18	L				
19	L				
20	L				
21	R				
22	R				
23	R				
24	R				
25	R				
26	R				
27	R				
28	R				
29	R				
30	R				
31	R				
32	R				
33	L				
34	L				
35	L				
36	L				
37	R				
38	R				
39	R		Notes/Reminders		
40	L				
41	L				

Fig 245

The vertical columns on the script from left-to-right include:

1. The play number in the period
2. The hash mark we snap the ball from
3. Specific situations (goal line, 3rd and 10, etc.) (D & D means down and distance) or quarterback rotations. Quarterback rotations are important for coaches who run specific plays or packages with specific players. For example, if our wide receiver coach wants to work timing between our top receivers and quarterback the script lets him know exactly when to bring the groups together.
4. Personnel, formation and play
5. Scout team front
6. Scout team blitz or line game

7.   Scout team coverage

Playbook, Video Cut-ups & Other Teaching Tools

Offensive coordinators are responsible for creating the playbook, preparing video cut-ups, and readying any other teaching tools before training camp begins. Large amounts of time are required when preparing new teaching or organizational tools. The goal is to first train the coaches properly before they pass on the learning. The next illustration (Figure 246) is a page from one of our playbooks.

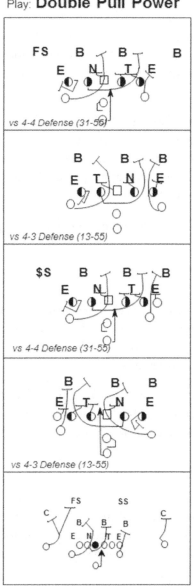

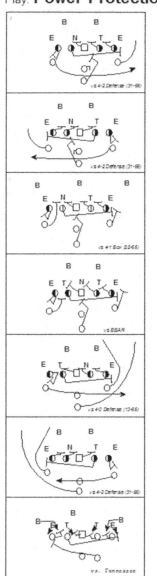

Fig 246

There are many different ways to design and layout an offensive playbook. We use both printed and digital playbooks. There are lots of different ways to use a playbook based on personal preferences and learning styles of your players. I feel that playbooks work best as overviews. Our playbook in particular is a cursory look at our offense. The players take notes to supplement the overview and learn through repetition in practice.

The playbook sample on the previous page shows both our Double Pull Power play and our Power Pass Protection. This info is all the players receive for these two schemes in terms of playbook content. It is up to the players to fill in all the blanks.

We do not provide charts and specific illustrations detailing the assignment for each player. We prefer for our players to come to this knowledge individually. This makes the learning more relevant and meaningful. It is one thing to see a play drawn up in a playbook—that type of learning is memorization. It's something totally different when a player visualizes and internalizes how the play works on the field—that's practical application. We want our players thinking in terms of all 11 men as part of a cohesive offensive scheme instead of memorizing what they do individually in isolation of the entire play and schematic concept. Learning entire play concepts is meaningful learning. Simply memorizing responsibilities for one position is inadequate.

Imagine for a moment a new offensive lineman on your team. He learns just before the start of fall camp that he's playing center. We do not want him to thumb through the playbook, trying to memorize just what the center does. Instead, we want him to look at each play as an integrated, coherent scheme and learn how all of the offensive players work together to execute the play. It is important that our players learn schematic concepts in their entirety. This is why we keep our playbooks at the "fly-over" level.

We want the players to make their own meaningful connections. These meaningful connections promote ownership of performance and better execution.

Staff Installation Meetings

An offensive coordinator must also make sure his coaches are ready to teach. A series of meetings are required where the offensive staff gets together to review each scheme and how it's being taught. Methods of teaching, how concepts are labeled/communicated, and how players train are decided ahead of time. From there the offensive staff plans out specific drills and teaching strategies.

Coaching point: offensive coordinators/head coaches need to allot adequate time to teach and drill everything the players must know. Part of this process involves creating a plan for how practice is monitored by the coaching staff. It is critical that coaches know where to focus their attention and what their specific role is during practice before starting of fall camp.

Personnel Analysis

Personnel analysis and assessment is an essential component of effective coaching. Teams need a plan in the pre-season for player rotations and the number of repetitions each player receives. A separate plan is also needed for where players are training/conditioning in terms of position groups.

Coaches must consider how many reps each player needs to reach adequate game shape. For a returning senior you probably know their training needs by position and previous experience. Based on this information you decide how many reps this player needs to be game ready and in game shape. Sometimes there are players you do not want taking many reps in training camp because your goal is making sure they are healthy and ready for the first game. The concern in this case is making sure they get just enough reps to execute at their highest level come game day.

All teams must create a football-specific plan to get their players into game shape. Hopefully your strength and conditioning coach is involved in designing this plan (in the NCAA this is required). This plan includes your pre-season conditioning specifications for each player and position group. It also includes your pre-season condition test designed to give a baseline of overall team and individual conditioning.

It's unrealistic to expect that players are ready to play a full game on the first day of pre-season practice. This is why a conditioning plan needs to work as a progression targeted at the first game. A good conditioning plan is tailored for each individual position group as well as the players inside the cohort.

When teams use running backs in four-play rotations they need specific training to reach full speed for four plays in a row. Similarly, offensive linemen who are not part of a rotation require a specialized training progression preparing them for 11 to 12 play drives.

We generally start players off with just a few reps at a time in the preseason. During training camp we slowly increase the number of plays until they reach the number we expect them to execute consecutively in a game. This is especially important with larger athletes such as offensive lineman. Linemen conditioning programs require deliberate training methods often different from other position groups. They should start with 2 to 4 play sets in fall camp before building to 8 to 12 sets on game week.

Position changes are possible for players at all levels of football. To do so effectively requires coaches to begin the season with a well-articulated plan for which players potentially play what positions. Sometimes position changes are happy accidents stumbled upon during practice and games. Other times a position change is necessitated by injuries or other factors. A specific, strategic plan is needed at the beginning of the season that prepares players in a manner best suited for the team's needs regardless of whether you are training a new starter or building depth for the future.

Unit & Position Meeting Plans

An offensive coordinator must also plan for what schemes are installed as a unit and which ones are installed as a position group. We install all formations as a unit for example. Anything related to eleven players working together is installed as a unit.

By operating this way we assure continuity in the message delivered to players. To supplement the message we do film review as an entire team. Bringing the entire offense together with the head coach and offensive coordinator to deliver instruction and provide feedback is enormously valuable. Top down messaging about what we are doing and how we are going to do it is an important aspect of continuity.

In the pre-season we also decide what groups are meeting separately and what groups are meeting together. There are lots of choices in regards to dividing players for meetings. Staffing and facilities allowing every position group to meet separately is an option for some teams. You may not find this an advantageous way to meet even if the space and staff is available however. Ultimately it's contingent on player and teaching needs.

There are times where I want to meet with the quarterbacks alone for example. This allows me to get into nuanced details about what our quarterbacks need to do. There are also times when I want to meet with the quarterbacks and wide receivers together. This makes sense because there is a great deal of information that pertains to both position groups. Meeting together saves time and emphasizes common themes. Details like route and player spacing, read progressions, attacking coverage, identifying coverage, etc. pertain to both position groups.

Meeting together is a much more efficient method of relaying information pertaining to multiple position groups. It also assures that everyone is coached the same way and is given the same message. Our running backs and offensive linemen often meet together for the same reasons quarterbacks and receivers do.

Subdividing position groups is also an option. We split our inside wide receivers and wings into a smaller group separate from split ends for example. We do this because both groups require different skills and different instruction. We constantly look for the best hybrid strategy of delivering information to full groups when it makes sense and delivering detailed specific information to small groups when it makes sense.

The offensive coordinator must also decide who is leading each meeting. It is important that communication is as smooth and consistent as possible. This includes creating an agenda for each meeting. The coach selected to lead the meeting must possess the technical knowledge requisite for directing instruction. A plan is also needed for any audiovisual and print materials needed. This potentially includes cut-up lists, printed playbooks, printed handouts, etc.

Walk-Through Plans

Walk through plans are extremely important—especially in college football where two-a-day practices are prohibited. We do a variety of activities during our walk-throughs including individual and multiple position group reviews respectively. Our quarterbacks/receivers and running back/linemen groups often work together during walk throughs. At the end we gather all position groups together and walk through plays with all eleven players.

We find there are other advantages in (1) splitting the offense into two groups or (2) rotating the offense through different groups. Some days we split our older and younger players for example. This allows us to work at a faster pace with the veteran players and a slower pace with newer ones. Learning through observation is also important to us. There are days where freshman and sophomores watch our juniors and seniors model skills or plays. It's critical for younger players to see what our offense looks like when executed the right way.

Practice Assignments for Each Coach

The importance of setting up a plan for each coach's area of emphasis in practice was previously mentioned. Concentrating on what each coach is supposed to do is made easier by outlining the players they are responsible for before practice begins.

Young coaches in particular are easily distracted. They get caught looking at the ball, a different position group, or any number of things they don't need to focus on. It is critical that players receive the attention they deserve. To do this we create a clear plan of who is monitoring what aspect and what group in practice.

Position Group Divisions

Position groups are dividable in the Tex-Bone offense. When coaching by position we teach based on the following groups: offensive line, tight ends, quarterbacks, inside wide receiver/wings, outside wide receivers, and fullback/running backs.

We subdivide our wide receivers because their job descriptions vary depending on situation, scheme, or scenario. There are times when we train entire position groups together given the general overlap of their responsibilities. Running backs are one group we do not always subdivide. We do sometimes subdivide our running backs into spread running backs and fullbacks however.

Scout Team Operation & Coordination

Scout team operation and coordination is an aspect often overlooked by many teams. We want our scout team operation to run smoothly for two reasons:

1. We want a positive experience for our developmental players. We want them to feel important and that what they do is valuable. We want them to see that coaches put time into planning what they do during practice. They need to see how important their roles are in team success.
2. We want efficiency. We want to move from play-to-play and drill-to-drill in a deliberate manner that does not waste time. To do so the scout team plan (including play wristbands, scout cards, etc.) must contain opponent-specific details so we perform at a high level on game day.

IN-SEASON DUTIES FOR THE
OFFENSIVE COORDINATOR

Video Cut-Ups & Other Teaching Tools

Offensive coordinators must develop a plan for video cut-ups and other teaching tools. This does not necessarily mean that he is the person producing all of this content. The person responsible for the production and duplication of teaching tools depends on the staff and the resources available. The offensive coordinator needs a plan to make sure that various tasks get done, taking into account any limitations. Trade tapes need analyzing, opponent video play lists need sharing, practice film needs sharing, handouts for players need producing, scouting reports need creating and producing, etc. This large flow of information needs coordination in a systematic manner.

Planning Opponent Analysis

Video analysis is a big deal in modern football. This is potentially one of the most important processes for a football team. There are many ways to analyze the tendencies of opponents. Modern video editing programs are excellent at producing numbers (statistics) and video cut ups that help analyze the tendencies of opponents. There are also outside companies that provide quality data as well.

Game planning begins with the compilation of data and a discussion among the staff. This is something we like to do as an entire staff—not just coordinators and the head coach. In these meetings we look at opponent personnel and situational tendencies that factor into how we play. Through video analysis and tendency analysis we compile short lists of plays we want to use. We also devise ways to use our player personnel in certain situations. In the final phase we plan for game specific situations (such as third down, red zone, backed up, or goal line for example).

Delegation is important. The offensive coordinator must learn to use the talents of all his coaches to make the offense operate efficiently. Assignments delegating exact responsibilities for each position coach are required. Who is compiling the scouting report? Who is producing cut-ups? Who is scripting practice segments? These questions are answered by properly assigning duties among the coaching staff.

Personnel Analysis

Personnel analysis needs a specific plan because it's ongoing and every-changing. Doing so properly requires a personnel plan for both games and practices. These plans must include skill advancement and player health considerations.

Coaching staffs generally do not overlook in game personnel groupings and substitution packages. Plans for practice rotations and substitutions are often the details that do not get as much attention however.

We carry as many as ten personnel groups into games. Preparing for this takes a tremendous amount of personnel analysis. The upside is that we only ask players to fill roles they are good at. This planning is worth the time investment.

Daily Practice Emphasis for Team Period

The Tex-Bone gives coaches multiple schemes, formations, and personnel groupings to choose from. The choices are not so many that a team cannot practice them all in one week if a daily theme is selected.

We work on 1st and 10 against a base defense during team period (11-vs-11) on Monday. This is done because we generally face an opponent's base defense on 1st and 10. Forty percent or more of plays during a game are 1st and 10 situations where you see an opponent's base defense a majority of the time.

On Tuesday we place an emphasis on rehearsing 3rd down situations. This gives us a chance to see blitzes and line games that we stand to face in short yardage situations versus an upcoming opponent. Third down is a make or break game situation. Practicing these situations on Tuesday leaves time for us to change the initial game plan if we don't like it.

On Wednesday we work on red zone and goal line. Even though red zone plays do not occur with great frequency during a game we still want to maximize our chances to score. We finished previous seasons as high as second in nation in red zone efficiency.

Thursday is our off day. Friday we work on our opening script and review game plan situations. Sometimes we revisit red zone or goal line (practiced earlier in the week) on Friday. This last practice before game day gives us the opportunity to practice every situation twice if necessary.

An important component of our Friday is we practice exactly 24 hours before kickoff (whenever possible). We find it beneficial to get our players focused on execution exactly one day before the game. If we are playing a 6:00 PM game on Saturday evening, we want practice at 6:00 PM on Friday. This plan is routed in Kinesiology.

Sub-Plans for Other Practice Periods

We use micro-plans for various practice periods throughout the season. During individual and inside run drills on Tuesday we work the triple option. On Wednesday we practice our spread elements, Jet Motion, and shifts/other motions. During 7-on-7 we work on passes against zone defenses on Tuesday and passes versus man coverages on Wednesday.

Practice Script

Practice scripting takes on additional importance during the season. There are a limited amount of reps in practice to get everything covered. Creating themes for each day allows the play caller and the scripter to keep pace with demands. It's difficult to run all of the plays, from all of formations, with all the desired personnel groups in practice without a script.

Individual Period Planning

Individual period plans are equally important during the season. Generally position coaches create these micro-plans. Similar to practice scripts it is important to analyze the amount of time needed for individual skill and group work. These plans are tailored to our daily practice emphases. The offensive coordinator must make sure he is including the amount of time his players need each day for individual skills into the practice plan if the head coach is not part of offensive planning sessions.

Unit & Position Meeting Planning

Knowing what is reviewed, what is taught, and who is leading the unit and position group meetings is vitally important. It needs planning out ahead of time. All of the considerations regarding unit and position group planning during the season are the same as what was discussed for pre-season planning.

Walk-Through Planning

We like our pre-practice walk-through to serve as a preview for the daily emphasis selected. Inside the walk-through we also want to address anything new. When asking players to execute a new play we want to give them the chance to run it at half speed first.

Preparing the Scouting Report & Game Menu

The practice plan template presented earlier in the chapter does not change much from pre-season to in-season. We fill it out with as much detail as possible day in and day out. We talk about and list our walk-through emphasis. We list a theme for team period and 7-on-7 as well. We plan everything our players do during each period.

CHAPTER 21: GAME PLAN CONSIDERATIONS & READY LISTS

TEX BONE ADVANTAGES (REVIEW)

Let's review some of the benefits of the Tex-Bone before examining some considerations a play caller needs to make before creating a game plan.

- The Tex-Bone offers modern advances to time tested schemes. The system provides a great deal of flexibility to tailor what you do with your personnel and opponents characteristics.
- Spread-based defenses use predictable alignments that are often vulnerable to triple option. This is the strength of the triple option compared with one-back spread formations.
- Blitzing and twisting line games are dissuaded by option schemes. Dealing with less defensive pressure and line movement is a big advantage the Tex-Bone creates.
- The Tex-Bone is unpredictable and hard to defend. Every play features spread or option looks.
- "Stop the option" defensive strategies lead to big plays in the play-action passing game.
- Runs and passes look identical in the Tex-Bone. The more time a team spends trying to play the option, the less time they spend on pass defense.
- The Tex-Bone gives you two offenses with one set of players. We run traditional triple option schemes from multiple formations. We also retain spread elements.
- The only limit to the Tex-Bone is your imagination.

USE YOUR ADVANTAGES

Play callers must use their team's advantages when game planning. Defensive responses to the Flexbone formations are tough to predict. The rules-based nature of the Flexbone makes responses easier to devise however.

Unpredictability is what makes running the Flexbone both good and bad. Opponents plan for the Flexbone in their own way. This plan is not seen ahead of time because the Flexbone is so unique. Chances are there is not another option team running the Flexbone in your conference. With that consideration in mind, an offensive coordinator wants to make the opponent defend the Flexbone option on their terms.

Incorporating the Flexbone into the game plan forces your opponents to spend valuable time planning and practicing to stop it. This means less practice time for stopping other aspects of the Tex-Bone.

Remember, you are probably better at running your Flexbone offense that your opponent is at defending it. That being said, the rest of the Tex-Bone is still at your disposal even if an opponent is successfully countering the Flexbone.

Being better at the executing Flexbone than the defense is at preventing it is usually (but not always) the case. We played the eventual national champion the year before this was written. Their personnel were better than ours at most positions. Their size, skill, and speed helped them slow the Flexbone. We earned chunks of yardage from our other Tex-Bone formations (the triple option specifically) after the Flexbone was neutralized.

Remember, the Flexbone is one triple option variant in the Tex-Bone offense. The system adapts well to spread formations as well. Most teams apply their base defense rules to the triple option instead of reinventing the defense for a single week. This is true against any formation a team runs the Tex-Bone out of. Time constraints for opponents are doubled given the uniqueness of the Tex-Bone overall and the nearly insurmountable challenge of scheming for every Tex-Bone triple option look (Flexbone, spread, etc.).

There is simply not enough time during a week of game planning for defenses to create a complete response to all your Tex-Bone variations. The advantage of this scenario is twofold: (1) opponents generally use base defenses against this unfamiliar offense which (2) makes offensive game planning slightly easier and more effective because an offensive coordinator knows a base defense is most likely coming.

This does not mean that defenses take a "roll the dice" attitude however. Opponents attempt to adapt their base defense to make it option sound by studying formations on film, looking for tendencies, and creating scout team looks during the week. All defenses develop a zone read philosophy that they expand to defend the triple option. This predictability is highly advantageous. Offensive coordinators are able to identify and exploit who takes the dive, who takes the quarterback, and who takes the pitch.

Other teams are likely to get film of your earlier opponent's defensive schemes against Power Read and Zone Read. This is not necessarily a disadvantage though. The defenses other teams ran against your offense earlier in the year are likely duplicated by future opponents. A weekly game plan is then built around this knowledge.

Remember, modern defenses are geared toward stopping one-back offenses with plays that are not blocked for touchdowns. Safeties are free runners against most one-back teams. These unblocked defenders are used to moving free in space to make tackles. Defensive coaches do not want to change how their safeties play through the alley. This knowledge allows you to predict how an opponent's safeties are going to play the triple option (taking the pitch man or the quarterback in the pitch phase).

OPPONENT ANALYSIS

I prefer to start game plan preparations with an analysis of the opponent's base defense. Doing this gives me a better understanding of their overall defensive philosophy. Knowing an opponent's philosophy is important for a Tex-Bone coach. It helps you accurately predict how a defense aligns against the triple option. The first step in that process is learning their philosophy against the spread.

I like to watch an opponent based on down and distance next. What do they do on Third Down and Fourth Down? How often do they adjust what they do on 1st and 10? These are important factors to research and become familiar with.

After that I study an opponent based on common game situations. How do they change based on field position? What game situations cause them to change? What field zones cause them to change their defense? What do they do when a team is backed up? What do they do when a team is inside their 5-yard line?

The next step is studying pressure tendencies. When do they blitz and why did they blitz? What players do they like to blitz with?

In the final step I research other clues that reveal how they plan to defend the Tex-Bone. Looking at how they react to motion is one example. It is important to ascertain what advantages are gained by motioning when creating a game plan.

An offensive coordinator might look at previous games against an opponent as a separate study. It doesn't matter if your previous teams ran Tex-Bone or not. This information informs you about how they put together a defensive game plan. It's valuable to revisit how an opponent lined up against your formations in previous years.

Follow the trail of information you uncover and follow your instincts. Watching film and looking at cut-ups reveals advantages. Go down a rabbit hole if you find one! It is common to find an edge you didn't know was there until an in depth opponent study is made. We are always looking for "outside of the box" ways to gain an advantage in preparation for our opponents. Sun Tzu in *The Art of War* wrote know the opponent as well as you know yourself. The same is true in football.

Checklist of Considerations

We use a checklist of considerations when game planning. The list contains all our base runs and passes. This includes the Flexbone, spread formations, and empty formations (both Flexbone and spread). We take into consideration what plays we like to run, what plays are we good at, and what plays best fit our personnel this week. From these considerations we create a base list of plays to start the game plan with.

An offensive coordinator is able to decide what plays to include in the weekly game plan based on this list. A smaller list of game planned runs and passes is then created from the larger base list. Everything in the Tex-Bone is rule based. This makes any play in the offense available against almost any defense. We still want to put plays into the game plan that are specifically designed to take advantage of an opponent even though most of our offense is adaptable to any defensive look. These new plays are not necessarily brand new for the week. Often they are familiar plays ran with a different look. Formations are also made new by introducing different motions. Personnel grouping changes also present the opportunity to make a familiar play different for an upcoming opponent.

We like to put special plays into each game plan. These are new plays unknown to our opponent. (They are unknown in terms of not showing up on traded film or were not used against an opponent in previous years.) We sometimes use a reverse, a double pass, or an unbalanced formation. There are lots of choices in terms of special plays. Legendary San Francisco 49ers coach Bill Walsh was an advocate of special or "trick plays." His advice was run your trick play before the opponent does. The surprise factor gives your team an edge. We certainly like gaining an edge against opponents with new or special plays. Our game plan details specific situations where the new plays for the week are most advantageous. Sometimes we hold special plays as a wildcard too.

We also look to see what others teams did against our opponent successfully. We check to see if schemes that worked for other opponents are related to a Tex-Bone scheme already in place. Sometimes we put an opponent's actual play into our offense if it was extremely successful against the team we face that week.

OFFENSIVE COORDINATOR GAME PLAN DUTIES

Scouting Report

The first thing to consider in game planning is the scouting report for players. Our scouting reports include:

- A cover page with some sort of "rah-rah" statement or quote. This "bulletin board" material is something to pique player interest and give them a little bit of extra extrinsic motivation to start the week.
- Information about the opponent's two-deep roster. Height, weight, and other basic information are important to include.
- A section of special notes, instructions, or rules. We put this at the beginning of the report because these are the details we want our players to see early in the week. These are ideas we revisit throughout the week. We want players thinking about them as they prepare.
- A plan for personnel groups. We use as many as 10 personal groups per game when running the Tex-Bone. We do this because it is critical to only ask players to do what they are good at. We do not want to put players in a position to fulfill a role they are not well suited for.
- Diagrams of the opposing defense. This includes their base fronts, base coverages, base blitzes, and base defensive line games. We want to give our players a visual representation of the opponent's defense for study purposes. This lets them know how we plan on lining up that week and what they should expect in response.
- Diagrams of our plays against their defense. The time invested in creating basic diagrams of our base plays against the opponent's defense is well worth it. Generally this is not an extensive time commitment given our staff's familiarity with our base offense. The payoff is great for our players. It is a useful reference guide for players as they study an opponent and visualize their performance.

Our scouting report is:

- Rules to dictate execution. We try to make the weekly game plan simple, clear, and concise for players.
- Solutions to problems. It tells players what to do if an opponent does not play base defense. This information informs quarterback decision-making in particular. Quarterbacks meet with the offensive coordinator during the week to go over the game plan in detail.
- Information to prepare players for what the opponent is likely to do in specific situations. We include diagrams of the opponent's base defense and how we block against them.
- An on-the-fly playbook. When adding new plays, motions, formations, or looks for the week we want to make sure players are provided clear diagrams and instructions about how to execute these new demands.

Our scouting report is not:

- More information than players need to comprehend the game plan. Our scouting report is typically six to eight pages—maybe ten at the most. We do not want to overload our report with minutia that causes player hesitation on game day.
- Charts and graphs chalked full of percentages and statistics. Charts, graphs, and percentages are useful for play callers but a distraction for players. Does your quarterback need to search his memory to recall blitz on third down statistics as he comes to the line of scrimmage in a critical situation? The answer is probably not. This statistic is important to the play caller, not the quarterback. He needs to know what to do if a blitz is encountered in this situation. Does the quarterback need to make a check? Does he know what checks are good against pressure? Our goal is not to clutter any player's brain (especially the quarterback) with erroneous or excessive information. Over thinking often leads to mistakes and slower game play. We only give our players the information they need to play aggressively and react instinctively against an opponent.

Personnel Analysis

The offensive coordinator needs to develop a plan for rotations and reps in both practice and game situations. This plan also needs to include specific personal groupings and substitutions.

We favor numbering our personnel groups rather than using traditional 10, 11, or 21 designations. This allows us to carry multiple personnel groups for the same formation. We often use two or three different Flexbone personnel groups for example. Our personnel groups are created around players more than formations. This is different than how most teams look at personnel groupings. On top of our base personnel groups we also create single player personnel tags to modify a specific player or position in a group. This is advantageous in a third and short or goal line situation.

Figure 247 shows a personnel page from a scouting report. On this diagram there are nine personnel group options. (There is no number five.) We fill in the opponent at the top. Then we drop our players into a two-deep chart so they know what personnel groups they are part of and what positions they are playing.

The first group on the personnel page is Jet motion or other motion plays. Group two is for split back formations and three is for one-back spread formations. The fourth and sixth groups are for Flexbone formations. Group seven is for Flexbone with a tight end and group eight is for empty formations. The ninth and tenth groups are for 2x1 open formations with a single wing.

"Opponent"- Personnel									
Pos	**1** Jet/Motion	**2** Split Backs	**3** Spread	**4** Flexbone	**6** Flexbone	**7** TE Flexbone	**8** Em. Flexbone	**9** Single Wing	**10** Single Wing
X									
2nd X									
F									
2nd F									
H / FB									
2nd H / FB									
Z									
2nd Z									
Y (TE)									
2nd Y									

Fig 247

These groupings change from week to week. Some weeks we use more than two Flexbone personnel groups. Other weeks we use more one-back spread personnel groups. It all depends on the opponent and the game plan.

We group players that work best in various formations instead of creating groups that align to specific formations. The sixth personnel group (Flexbone) also works well in spread formations. Our emphasis is on grouping players for formations. The goal is to get as many players involved in game plans and personnel groups as possible. Players who are ready for varsity action see the field. We are able to do this because of our focus on player strengths. We don't need players that fit all roles—we need ones who fit specific rolls.

PLAY CALLER'S MENU: the "Ready List"

There are many different ways to organize a play-calling menu. I've used them all at some point over the years. It's important for a play caller to review what's working for them currently while considering what changes are needed in the future.

The following are essential components of the Tex-Bone play-calling menu. They include:

- Runs and passes by formation. Much of what the Tex-Bone does involves understanding how teams align to our different formations.   This makes it logical to group the ready list based on formation. Listing plays based on formation gives quick information access when a defense gives looks that were anticipated during the week.   Arranging the menu this way is also valuable because it provides information on how plays in a formation are potentially affected by defensive looks that were not anticipated in the game plan.
- The menu must contain offensive responses and counterattacks. The play caller must anticipate what the defense might do differently and have responses ready to counter it.
- Opening (possession or possessions) script. Are there formations you are almost certain you know what the defense alignment against them is? If yes, plan to attack that early. Naturally there are formations where you are not sure what defense you might see.   Working those formations into the game as early as possible is a good idea as well. This allows the offensive coaching staff to diagnose and respond to the defense moving forward.
- All game plan menus must account for specific game situations. You want plans for third and fourth down as well as sub-plans for red zone and backed-up scenarios.
- A list of "must call" plays. These are plays based on analysis you think are the "best of the best" elements of the game plan. They are the "go to" plays you expect to succeed. They are plays you want to make sure to call during the game.

The next illustration (Figure 248) shows one of our Tex-Bone ready lists. The far left side is a list of plays based on formation families. We put plays grouped by 2x1 formations in the top left. We highlight pass plays with a blue background and run plays with a green background. We also include groupings for 2x2 formations and 3x1 formations because we expect to know how the defense plans on lining up against them. Our plays are grouped overall according to our knowledge of how an opponent lines up against specific formations.

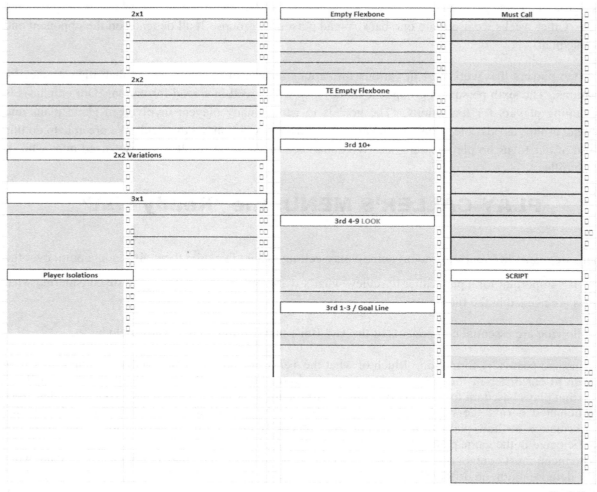

Fig 248

Next, we include a section for player isolations where the goal is to get the ball to specific player. In the middle area of the menu we put a plan for empty formations and empty Flexbone. Below that are groupings for specific situations. We divided our third down plan into three different situations: (1) third and 10 or more, (2) third and four to nine, and (3) third and one to three yards in the ready list above. These plays were grouped together on this ready list specifically because we felt our opponent's short yardage/goal line defense was similar to their third and 1 to 3 yards defense.

In the top right corner is our must call list. These are plays we felt were the best pieces of the game plan that we need to call during the game. In the bottom right corner is our opening script. This is a list of plays we want to look at early. Some of the lines on the opening script include two check boxes. That means if the play works well the first time we might consider coming back to it again before leaving the opening script.

Was Bill Walsh Right?

Bill Walsh is widely credited as the father of modern offensive game plans. A wide variety of Bill Walsh books and materials about game planning are available. Walsh invented the play caller menu we use today. The Walsh chart included a plan for every situation imaginable. His philosophy was that it's easier to make decisions in the office on Wednesday than it is to make decisions with the play clock running down on game day.

Was Bill Walsh right is the big question. How much is too much? When do you hit paralysis by analysis? When does a play caller get distracted by his chart and stop watching the game? What if the plays on the call sheet aren't working? These are all important considerations for a play caller to sort out.

Notice in the Tex-Bone menu on the last page there is not a written plan for what to do if we are up by 14 in the first quarter and it starts to rain. Bill Walsh created a section for this. I personally find that level of detail a bit too much. You decide for yourself.

An Alternative to the NFL Sized Menu

I suggest visualization exercises for play callers as an alternative to an NFL sized play menu. In doing this you pre-rehearse reactions to a wide variety of game situations and defensive countermeasures. That way if you are ahead early, down early, if it rains, if there is an injury, if you face a defense you didn't expect, or any of the other situation like this you know what to do. Visualization allows you to rehearse these scenarios and mentally map a response. Visualization keeps you calm and focused during the hectic and pressure filled nature of the game. Visualization exercises are strongly recommended for athletes as well.

The Tex-Bone structure alleviates some of these concerns over stressful in-game situations. Remember, the Tex-Bone is a rule-based system.   A large part of what Bill Walsh did on offense was game planned week to week at a genius level. This put pressure on the offensive coordinator to "reinvent the wheel" in certain circumstances. This is not to say that Walsh's ideas weren't innovative or influential—they certainly are. Our point examines Walsh's approach from a broader perspective, noting that no system is perfect.

The Tex-Bone System contains a reliable systematic structure. This frees an offensive coordinator from drawing up a brand new game plan every week. The fact that solutions to defensive pressure, line games, and multiple coverages are built into the system is a stress reliever for play callers.

Sideline vs. Pressbox Play Calling

There is a quiet and calmness to the press box. The press box also gives the best view of the action. There is room for materials including charts, diagrams, and notes. You are able to bring as many different colored markers or pens as needed. You also get room for as many cans of Diet Coke as you need.

The field is chaos by comparison. Sight lines are limited and there is no room for materials. Extra charts and diagram are not an option and you are basically limited to one pen. You are reliant on spotters with better sightlines and view of the game.

I recommend putting the play caller in the press box unless he is the head coach. The press box is a much more calm and quiet environment. It is a better location for analysis of the opponent and there are better sightlines. Is calling plays from the sideline an option? Certainly. I call plays from the sideline as the head coach. I readily admit it is a difficult situation that takes practice to perform effectively however. From the sideline you are reliant on assisting coaches. Play callers need to train coaches on how to spot for you in order to overcome these limitations.

CHAPTER 22: GAME DAY

COACHING STAFF ROLES & PRESSBOX CHARTS

That Must-Have Moving Pieces

The Play Caller: I suggest placing the play caller in the press box unless he is the head coach.

Field-Level Personnel: the field level needs a substitution and personnel communicator. This coach communicates with perimeter personnel groups between each series. A coach is also needed to communicate with the offensive line and running back personnel groups. I suggest placing the offensive line coach on the sideline in the roll of communicator with interior personnel. On a large staff the substitution and personnel communicators are different coaches potentially. With smaller staffs the substitution and personnel communicator often pulls double duty on the sideline.

It is important the play caller and the offensive line coach take different vantage points when both are on the field. The play caller generally stands close to the line of scrimmage, while the offensive line coach generally stands as far down the sideline as possible to gain a view from behind the action. Setting these two field-level vantage points is important for play caller and line coach communication throughout the game.

Press box: Coaches in the press box are the primary eyes for the play caller and offensive line coach. We place a coach who charts defensive tendencies and alignments in the press box as well.

Additional Staffing Assignments

Additional coaches are generally split between substitution and personnel communication duties on the field. Larger coaching staffs often put multiple spotters with specific jobs in the press box as well. One coach watches the defensive front and another watches the coverage for example. Dividing chart duties and expanding the amount of information collected in the press box is an advantage for larger coaching staffs.

Figure 249 shows a sample play chart for the offense. The play caller may want to reference what they ran before in terms of play combinations and formations. He may also want to know how many ways the offense ran a certain play or what plays the offense ran from a specific formation. This chart gives the offensive play caller a quick reference to the information he needs in terms of what plays were called previously.

2017 *Scrimmage* @ SAGU - ZW CALLSHEET

[illegible]	[illegible]	[illegible]	[illegible]	[illegible]	[illegible]	[illegible]	PLAY (1-25)	DEFENSE	NOTES
1									
2									
3									
4									
5									
6									
7									
8									
9									
10									
11									
12									
13									
14									
15									
16									
17									
18									
19									
20									
21									
22									
23									
24									

Fig 249

The next illustration (Figure 250) is an example of a press box chart used for tracking defensive alignment. Charting how the defense lines up gives us an accurate account of how the opponent defends each formation. Press box spotters are able to pre-populate the chart with expected defensive alignments once you develop your game plan for the week. We draw every formation to the left in our press box chart. Drawing your chart where one column is aligned strong left and the other strong right is also an option if that's what the spotter prefers.

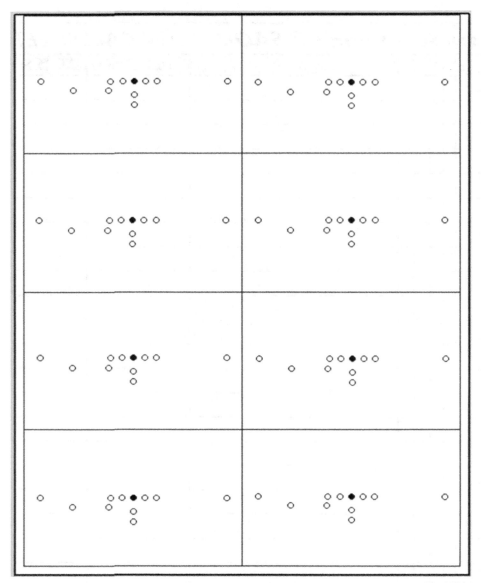

Fig 250

A spotter is able to pre-populate the chart with multiple alignments on the same page if you enter the game expecting a defense to line-up against a formation in two different ways. The spotter marks it one time if the defense runs an expected look. The rest of the chart is reserved for unexpected looks. The spotter quickly diagrams or makes notes covering what the defense is doing against a specific formation.

The play caller then talks to the spotter as needed between each series and asks questions about how the opponent is defending the formations used previously. This information guides the play caller when anticipating what he will see from the defense in the next series.

It is important that inexperienced play callers receive quality information from the spotters. Coaches learn to see the field more adroitly with experience. Even veteran play callers find spotters useful when they change to a new offensive system.

APPENDIX

Coaches, thank you for your interest in the Tex-Bone. Supplemental materials (including selected diagrams, power point slides, templates and excel documents) are available to original purchasers of this book. To gain access to these materials, please email me at coachjoeaustin@gmail.com.

If you have any questions while you are studying or implementing the Tex-Bone, please reach out. Coach Tom Ross and I are happy to help. God bless you and your team.

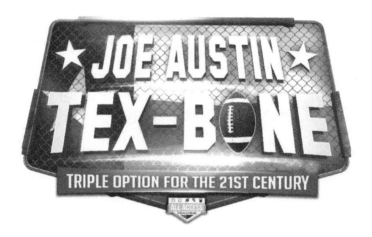